SILENCED PLEA

PLEA

The Child Who Learned Differently

KELLY VANZANT

Neuro Navigation Publishing
777 N. Jefferson Street
Milwaukee, WI 53202

TABLE OF CONTENTS

PREFACE

Have you ever had that feeling that something about you was different? Well, my feeling of being different because of my learning disabilities was almost the death of me.

The disabilities themselves were not the problem, but the way that everyone around me responded to my ability to learn differently left me isolated and feeling like I did not belong. Years of this evolved into a deep depression and contemplation of how to make the emotional pain stop for good.

I was relentlessly teased, isolated, and shamed in school because I could not read, write, or recognize my first name at age 14.

I have learning disabilities. On the one hand, I've come to appreciate that my specific disabilities give me a unique perspective. On the other hand, while in school, because learning disabilities are "invisible," I easily slipped through the cracks of the system, which prevented me from getting an education.

My learning abilities include dyslexia, dysgraphia, dyscalculia, and dyspraxia, and therefore, I am on the neurodivergent spectrum—to keep it simple, I'm someone who learns differently. It took me a long time to be okay with being me, but one of my biggest struggles was getting the public school system to accept me being me.

Through recognizing, accepting, and finding help for my disabilities, I unlocked a learning method that worked for my comprehension needs. Once that happened, it felt like a lightbulb had come on. The best way I can describe it is that it was like being in a haunted house where, one by one, I found the light switches that allowed me to remove the darkness, decrease the fear, and eventually take control of the nightmare.

Today, I am graduating college as an honor student recognized on the President's List and a member of the Speakers Association, The Society for Neurodiversity, and the Alpha Delta Lambda Honor Society.

This is my story. It is about what I went through, how I got the help I needed, and what I have achieved since receiving that help. It is difficult for me to tell this story because it brings back trauma, but I want to tell it in the hopes that others do not have to endure the path I was on for far too long.

I did not walk this journey alone; I have my mom to thank for never giving up on me, even when I briefly gave up on myself. We also carried each other through the journey of writing this book—and throughout the chapters, my mom provides her perspective on how we navigated the school system together to find success for my neurodiversity learning needs.

My story is unique to me. However, as I have shared it with others who are struggling, they have expressed gratitude for not feeling alone and have found hope through my experiences and success. Knowledge is power, and my goal is that you—the reader—will find my story and the information within this book helpful. May you also find the illuminating switch that brightens your learning journey.

My mom and I could not have put together this body of work without the help of experts—we pulled from the most recent research in the field. We have added a research section within each chapter to recognize the excellent work in this field. As part of sharing my journey and experiences, we also felt it was valuable to share the nuggets of information we discovered along the way. These are not items that can be found in a textbook or article; they're the real "aha!" moments that we were lucky enough to stumble upon during our journey. As such, based on our discoveries, this book is also intended to be a resource for you.

Together, we hope to make the much-needed systemic change for neurodivergent learners everywhere!

WHAT YOU SHOULD KNOW

If your child is struggling in school, if their teachers report that your child is distracted or not showing enough effort, or if you wonder why your child spends hours on homework each night—it does not mean you have a bad kid, an uncaring teacher, or that you're a terrible parent. It might mean that your child is a neurodivergent learner stuck in a school system set up for neurotypical learners. Your child may need different tools and information to find their academic success. We want to help.

Because this story could be *your* story, it could also be the solution you will *not* find in the school system.

WHO THIS BOOK IS FOR

Parents and caregivers of neurodivergent learners will gain a better understanding of the challenges faced by their children and discover strategies to support their educational journeys.

Educators and school administrators will read the book to gain insights into creating an inclusive and supportive learning environment for neurodivergent learners.

Neurodivergent learners will relate to this book, feel less alone, find inspiration, and discover strategies—like the value of self-advocacy—to succeed in their neurotypical school system.

INTRODUCTION

One of my most impactful experiences was sitting down with a guidance counselor in my senior year of high school. Three weeks before graduation, we discussed my future.

I had just told this guidance counselor I was considering completing a college application and wanted his assistance. What he said back to me was something I will never forget.

Through a blank stare, the counselor said, "Oh yeah, that's a good school, but that won't work for you. It would be best if you were more realistic with your expectations for yourself. Why don't you instead look for trade jobs or a city job like being a garbage collector because that would be more your speed"?

These words were not new to me; I'd heard them all my life—I still do—and they're hurtful every time.

The reason he said those things wasn't because I was struggling or failing in school. It was solely because I had learning disabilities, and he, like many others, saw little potential for success in my educational future because I learned differently.

I have hundreds of similar stories and know I'm not alone. Many friends, family members, acquaintances, and strangers who have walked the same path as me share similar experiences. I'm not unique or different—this way of thinking is a problem and one I'd like to see fixed.

Today, I am preparing to deliver my college commencement speech. I completed that college application without help, and not only did the college award me a scholarship, but I also excelled and was asked to provide a commencement graduation speech. I am nervous, but more than anything, this feels like a pivotal moment.

My black robe is perfectly pressed—and, unfortunately, is hiding my new size eight jumpsuit that I spent three hours picking out at the mall. My light brown, slightly wavy hair does what it wants, as usual, but at least it is tame under my graduation cap. For the first time since drama class, I'm wearing mascara to highlight my green eyes—an idea my mom had just before we left the house. Though I am five feet eight, for some reason, as I look from behind the curtains at the large audience gathering for the ceremony, I suddenly feel exceedingly small in my platform shoes. I cannot believe I am graduating college! I am thankful to be recognized as an honor student and to have been asked to speak at this event.

I don't think anyone—including me—could have predicted this moment even a few years earlier.

But here we are.

I hear the college president say, "Next is Kelly VanZant. Kelly is recognized for excelling in her studies while managing her specific learning disabilities. Kelly's story is incredible and inspirational! Without further ado, let's welcome Kelly to the stage."

I quickly pull up my robe so I don't trip as I emerge from behind the curtain and walk to the podium. I feel my butterflies turn into bees, and suddenly, I have beads of sweat on my forehead as I look upon the sea of people clapping in the audience. As soon as I get to the podium and adjust the mic, I feel a warm flush of positive energy throughout my body. This is my opportunity to speak up, advocate, and educate for a brighter future. I hear my voice amplified across the vast room as I smile and say:

"Ladies and gentlemen, esteemed faculty, proud parents, my fellow graduates, welcome to graduation day!"

YOU CAN TAKE CONTROL AND MAKE POSITIVE CHANGES!

CHAPTER 1

DIFFERENT FROM THE START:
EARLY CHILDHOOD EXPERIENCES

Before preschool, I went to Kidsplace a few days a week. It was like a prekindergarten where we played and did other activities with kids of the same age. I liked this place, and I recall that my time there began my memories of feeling different.

At Kidsplace, when it was quiet time, we each picked out a book and were given a space to read it. We sat on floor mats scattered across the main playroom, arm's length away from each other. While some kids read their books, I would watch for those kids who looked like they were done reading or not reading at all.

I slowly inched my mat to the kid next to me, whom I called "friend." I called almost everyone "friend" because I couldn't remember names. This was one of the few friends who was like me. He was much taller than me and had olive skin, hazel eyes, and short, curly hair. This friend was like me because he had wiggles, too, during quiet time.

I often had long and confusing talks with the daycare attendants at Kidspace about how I had unknowingly broken a rule. I remember a regular pattern of a daycare attendant pulling me aside to tell me that I hurt someone's feelings with my words, didn't follow directions, or needed to sit and think about my actions when I wasn't exactly sure what I had done.

Looking back, I feel that I had a tough time understanding these rules. And it seemed I was often not in the right place at the right time.

For example, I got time out one day in the dollhouse room because I was supposed to be in the activity room. I wasn't playing around; I was genuinely lost because I did not understand the directions or social signals to go to the next area.

I don't know if I was slow to process, self-absorbed in my world, or low functioning when it came to understanding directions, but I often felt like I couldn't connect the dots and be at the right place at the right time. I didn't know why, but I knew I was different.

I also cannot remember a time when I did not feel clumsy. For example, when Mom signed me up for a youth soccer team, I could never master foot-eye coordination. Heck, I still feel like I don't have coordination fully figured out. People around me seem to notice that, too—I often hear, "Be careful" and "Slow down." I am known to trip on the air around me.

My least favorite advice from grown-ups was, "Think before you act." How was I supposed to do that?

Because of my clumsiness, I've had a lot of accidents. Most were embarrassing but not too serious—like I would regularly spill my drink or trip on nothing—but sometimes they were painful. For example, when I was five years old, while visiting the local museum, I somehow managed to fall, going up a flight of stairs *and* breaking my arm in multiple places. I can't tell you how many times I've fallen going upstairs! Who falls going up the stairs?

About a year later, I got 28 stitches on my forehead while playing in one of those kid gerbil tube-like gyms. I was running around, going in one tube and out the other, and suddenly, I found myself falling and hitting my forehead on the top of a big yellow tube. I remember being scared, then not seeing or feeling anything, and then waking up with another kid screaming over me. I had blood all over my shirt and in my hair. The next thing I knew, I was in an ambulance headed to the hospital again.

My mom did her best to protect me, and I tried to be more careful, but it always seemed like I was just a clumsy kid. We didn't have a good answer for a long while as to why I was so accident-prone.

MOM'S PERSPECTIVE:

My pregnancy with Kelly was uneventful. Everything was identified as "normal" until it was time to deliver. My water broke about 9 p.m. and by 11 p.m. I was seeing small traces of meconium after I peed. This made the nurses and doctors nervous, and they decided to perform a C-section. A few hours later, Kelly was born. She was a gorgeous, hairless, round, eight-pound baby girl who looked like she was from a Pampers commercial.

Shortly after birth and after passing the standard hospital tests, including a state-mandated hearing test, Kelly and I left the hospital and headed home. Over the next year, Kelly hit every milestone of baby development and received great checkups during the myriad well-baby pediatrician visits.

All except one.

Kelly had a difficult time sleeping. After many tests, she was diagnosed with a sleeping disorder. Otherwise, she was a happy and curious child who loved to explore, see, touch, and sometimes taste new things. She treasured her bath time and playtime and enjoyed new food, and before long, she started to crawl, walk, talk, and sing! My goodness, this child still loves to sing every day.

When my maternity leave was exhausted, I returned to work. I was fortunate that one of the benefits of my employment was an on-site daycare. Every weekday I went to work, I would drop Kelly off at the daycare and take the elevator upstairs to my office.

The daycare staff were terrific; they adored Kelly and provided daily activity reports. When she was around one, they shared that her vocabulary was advanced. As she got older, the daycare reports often stated that she and her buddy Quinn played well together. However, during reading time, Kelly was distractive to others, so the staff frequently took her out of the room so others could listen to the stories. They shared that she found more joy in being active than sitting during reading time.

When we got home at the end of the workday, Kelly wanted to swing in the backyard. She often sang about her day and what she did, or sometimes she said she was teaching "Songa" what she had learned. For a short time before preschool, Kelly had an imaginary friend named Songa.

I understood that Songa was present primarily during eating, play, and reading hours. Kelly was serious about Songa, and I was too. At dinner time, she insisted that Songa have a plate of food, too, and I was happy to oblige. I appreciated Songa because she seemed to help Kelly sit for a bit longer as Kelly focused on eating with her.

After dinner, during story time, Kelly was less patient. She didn't want to sit in my lap and stare at a book. She wanted the page turned before the words were done being read. I started pointing at each word to show why I was still on the same page, and she would say, "Keep reading to Songa," as she got up and walked across the room to listen from afar while tinkering with something from her toybox.

Our picture books were short, and when I finished the story announcing "The End." As soon as I was done, Kelly would tell me that Songa didn't want to read anymore and invite her to the toy box to play.

As Kelly grew older, around the time kindergarten started, Songa left as suddenly as she had arrived. There was no announcement; she wasn't mentioned as much, and then, eventually, not at all. When school began, life started to get complicated.

Looking back, the signs we experienced make more sense now that Kelly's specific learning disabilities have been identified.

One sign was her consistent avoidance of reading time. Kelly would semi-tolerate being read to but was mostly interested in the pictures on the page. She didn't, however, tolerate reading a book more than once. When I completed a book, she would say, "All done," and then kindly take the book from my hands and place it in the trash bin.

Another area of uniqueness was her tactile sensitivity. She did not want her hair brushed, she didn't like hugs, and she was particular about clothes as they could be itchy especially the tags. She did love her bathtime, however. She found the limited tub space a reduction in distractions and the warm water sensory soothing.

I often referred to her as my wiggle worm, as she could not sit still for long, especially in restaurants, movies, or venues that require the social norm to sit, watch, and listen. She was always well-behaved, just wiggly as if her chair or outfit were uncomfortable.

Lastly, Kelly seemed to struggle with spatial judgment. For example, she would miss the table when attempting to return a cup to where she picked it up, not once but almost every time! I was concerned about this, so I took her to the eye doctor, and the optometrist said her vision was perfect. To this day, when she sits down, she plops, regardless of the potential consequences of a hard surface. When walking, she will turn around corners too early or bump her arm on objects that could have been avoided. We tried multiple times, but Kelly could never master riding her bike due to being unable to balance it.

One of Kelly's most challenging areas was her inability to get tired. Around 8 p.m. each night, her body seemed to do the opposite of relaxing; instead, she gained energy. This increasing energy turned into hyperactivity that she found exhausting—it still happens regularly, regardless of how tired she is. After several tests, it was determined she had a sleeping disorder. Her pediatrician prescribes her medicine that helps her get the rest she needs nightly. Her insomnia could result in her not sleeping for two or more days, causing her immune system to weaken and her mental health to suffer.

Some of these challenges have caused significant illness and injury. For example, Kelly's first ambulance ride was when she broke her arm in multiple places while walking up the first three steps of a staircase at a museum on a daycare field trip. After the arm had fully healed, her next ambulance trip ended in 28 stitches after falling inside a kids' jungle gym.

None of these outcomes were as damaging to her health as the isolation and feeling of not belonging while at public school.

Her extra sensitivity to physical touch, inability to sit for lengthy periods, lack of coordination, resistance to reading or learning letters, and exhausting insomnia in her first five years of life were unmistakable signs that things were different for Kelly. However, I was a new mom with my first child, and my understanding of Kelly's unique experiences of the unforgiving world around her was not as straightforward then as it is to me today.

Looking back on all she's been through, I am amazed at her patience, kindness, and strength. It's been tough for her, and it was especially so before she could explain that she was not experiencing the world in the same way that others around her were experiencing it. At times, it seemed the world was punishing her for being different.

RESEARCH INFORMATION:

Neurodivergence: The variety and diversity of thought and behavior

Neurodivergent is a term that medical and educational professionals use to describe the diversity and variations in human minds and how people think and perform, as the Cleveland Clinic explains.[1]

People who are neurodivergent have varied brain development or function for a variety of reasons. Genetics or heredity, environmental factors such as exposure to chemicals or poor nutrition, and traumatic brain traumas are some of the recognized causes of this. National Institute of Health research suggests meconium exposure has a connection to autism.[2]

According to the CDC, seven percent of people identify as neurodivergent.[3]

Neurodivergence and Specific Learning Disabilities:
According to the CDC, learning impairments and ADHD are the most common neurodivergent conditions. Seven percent of people identify as neurodivergent. The neurodivergent spectrum covers different kinds of clinically diagnosed differences, including a group called specific learning difficulties. Specific learning disabilities are persistent challenges in listening, thinking, writing, spelling, or doing math that interfere with learning.

Specific learning difficulties are usually diagnosed between three and 17 if they exist.[4] Kelly showed signs of dyslexia as early as first grade, but she did not get a diagnosis until she was nine. A national survey of parents revealed that more than 3.5 million children have dyslexia and attention problems.

Specific learning disabilities and other conditions like ADHD are protected disabilities under the Americans with Disability Act (ADA).[4] The medically recognized conditions that make up specific learning disabilities include:

- **Dyslexia:** A reading disorder that makes it difficult to read, write, and spell words

- **Dysgraphia:** A writing disorder that makes it difficult to write legibly and coherently

- **Dyscalculia:** A math disorder that makes it difficult to understand and solve mathematical problems

- **Dyspraxia:** a disorder that affects motor skills, coordination, and planning

- **Developmental aphasia:** a disorder that affects language, speech, and communication

THE CHILD WHO LEARNED DIFFERENTLY

Specific learning disabilities are not seen as bad, and treating the particular condition as soon as possible is essential to supporting and optimizing the learning capacity of people who learn differently and giving them learning equity in the classroom.

Neurodivergence and ADHD in Children:
ADHD, also known as attention deficit hyperactivity disorder, is a condition that involves hyperactive-impulsive behavior and difficulty paying attention.[5] The symptoms can vary from mild to severe and persist into adulthood. Research has shown that different genders may exhibit other signs of ADHD. For example, girls may be more likely to have quiet inattention, while boys may be more restless and energetic. Kelly had trouble concentrating and completing tasks since she was a toddler. She often got distracted and forgot what to do when she went to another room. She was later diagnosed with an inattentive type of ADHD.

It is important to note that ADHD does not cause other psychological or developmental problems. However, as with Kelly, children with ADHD are more likely than others also to have specific learning disabilities. Specific learning disabilities are distinct from attention deficit hyperactivity disorder (ADHD).

The neurodivergent brain usually has both strengths and disadvantages because of its way of functioning. Specific learning disabilities and ADHD don't make a person less intelligent or incapable of learning. However, teachers and parents must recognize a neurodivergent individual's unique learning style to improve the child's comprehension.

REFERENCES:

[1] Professional, Cleveland Clinic Medical. n.d. "Neurodivergent." Cleveland Clinic. https://my.clevelandclinic.org/health/symptoms/23154-neurodivergent.

[2] Ensiyeh Jenabi, Erfan Ayubi, Salman Khazaei, Saeed Bashirian, and Mojtaba Khazaei. 2021. "Is Meconium Exposure Associated With Autism Spectrum Disorders in Children?" Clinical and Experimental Pediatrics (Online) 64 (7): 341–46. https://doi.org/10.3345/cep.2020.01053.

[3] "Data and Statistics About ADHD | CDC." 2022. Centers for Disease Control and Prevention. June 8, 2022. https://www.cdc.gov/ncbddd/adhd/data.html.

[4] Individuals with Disabilities Education Act. 2024. "Individuals With Disabilities Education Act (IDEA)." March 15, 2024. https://sites.ed.gov/idea

[5] "What Is ADHD?" n.d. https://www.psychiatry.org/patients-families/adhd/what-is-adhd

ACTION ITEMS:

1. Observe your child's socialization skills.

2. Share concerns about your child's socialization skills with their pediatrician.

3. Continue to educate yourself, becoming familiar with the signs and symptoms displayed by neurodivergent learners.

LIKE A DIAMOND, YOU WILL SHINE BRIGHTEST IN YOUR LEARNING STYLE ELEMENT.

CHAPTER 2

NAVIGATING THE CLASSROOM: EARLY PUBLIC SCHOOL YEARS

I was excited about starting school—especially since the neighbor kids next door always talked about the fun they had during recess.

Mom and I counted down the days before school started. Sometimes, I would think about school while in bed at night, trying to fall asleep. I might meet a friend with a swimming pool or someone who likes to climb trees. There was so much I was looking forward to at this kids' place called school.

The first day of school finally arrived, and a long yellow bus picked me up at the corner across from my house. I wore my favorite purple t-shirt with galloping horses printed across the front. I wore my most comfortable no-button blue jeans and new purple no-lace Sketchers. My matching purple backpack was big for my body, but it was light because it only had my Nutella banana sandwich, a carrot, an apple, a juice box, and a small bag of my favorite—Sour Patch Kids inside. My brown shoulder-length hair was messy from sleeping on it, but my freshly cut bangs were neat and straight as they framed my face.

I waved bye to Mom, climbed the tall steps of the bus, and quickly sat in the first seat behind the driver.

It was a bumpy ride, and the bus had a strange smell that made my stomach sick, but it was also fun. At the next stop, more kids got on, and a girl sat next to me. We did not speak as we glanced at each other. After a few more stops, the quiet bus was filled with kids talking and laughing. I looked at the girl sitting next to me and smiled. She did not smile back. Suddenly, we encountered a big bump that sent both of us bouncing in our seats, eliciting a collective "WHOA!" from everyone on the bus! The girl in the same seat as me exchanged glances once more, and this time, we burst into laughter.

A teacher met us when I got off the bus, and I went to my classroom.

I was ready for school to be fun. There were a lot of kids in my class, and they seemed happy to be there. They were smiling and talking as they looked around the classroom. The teacher said there were 30 desks and that we should find our seats. The teacher told me my desk was in the back because my last name started with the letter "V." Soon, as I sat down, the classroom felt even more gigantic, as the teacher was way up front.

My big classroom had two large windows facing the playground, colorful carpet tiles in the middle of the room that made a giant rainbow, and every wall was jam-packed with different pictures or symbols. The room had bright white lights, and by lunchtime, they made my eyes feel like I had been staring into the sun. I sat under-neath a clock that constantly made a "tick" sound. A loud hum from a tiny fish tank was on the opposite side of the room. The tank had one floating plastic plant, neon green gravel, and a beautiful red and orange Betta fish the teacher called Bert.

But every day, school got a little more confusing. Because we were the youngest class, we could not go to the playground, which I was most excited about. Instead, we had recess in the gym. We spent much of our time inside listening to stories and doing activities like tracing letters and numbers. I didn't understand why we did this instead of going outside.

The classroom presented problems. The lights were so bright that my eyes and head hurt by the end of the day. I swear I could hear the lights buzzing, but when I asked others if they heard it, they thought I was joking. We did a lot of sitting at our desks, which was hard for me. My legs felt jumpy when they hung down for a long time. I also found my seat to be slippery, and this caused me to slide down and almost off when I adjusted. When I pulled my legs up underneath me to stop the sliding, my teacher told me to sit correctly in my chair with both feet on the ground. I found this request to be impossible, but I still tried.

One day, a teacher came to my desk and told me I had to join her in the hallway. I followed her from my classroom to the hall. We walked to the end of the long hall where other kids and a special teacher sat. I sat in the only open desk and joined this new group. I wasn't sure why, but I was asked to sit at a desk in the hallway daily. I found out later this was part of a "special class time." I noticed that while in the hall, we each worked on different assignments. The hall teacher watched us while we did our work. She said she was there if we had questions, but she always looked busy working on a bunch of papers, so I tried not to bother her.

I had a hard time explaining things with this special hallway teacher. For example, I told her maybe I was allergic to the paper because it made me itch. Without looking up, she said there was no such thing as being allergic to paper. She told me I was lazy and didn't want to do the work. On a different day, I tried to tell her that rubbing the pencil lead onto the paper made my hand tingle. She looked up from her papers and called me a liar, making me feel bad. I started to cry but knew I couldn't leave, so I walked to the other side of the hall and wiped away the tears before they reached my chin. The hallway teacher didn't seem to care and just said I should return to my desk when I was ready. This situation was embarrassing, and it hurt my feelings. I decided not to tell her anything else.

MOM'S PERSPECTIVE:

At the time, I was not aware that Kelly had specific learning disabilities. I had not heard of dysgraphia, dyspraxia, and dyscalculia, let alone know what traits they might exhibit that would allow one to detect their presence. Kelly was eventually diagnosed with dyslexia and ADHD, but at the time, I understood that these conditions were more known to be diagnosed in boys and very rarely seen in girls.

Looking back on what I know today, one key area I would have focused my attention on more was Kelly's socialization patterns. Before school started, Kelly was outgoing and not shy about starting conversations with strangers. However, she struggled with developing small talk skills, seemed to use literal concepts predominately, and became confused with jokes or sarcasm.

For example, one day, a new neighbor was unloading boxes from a U-Haul truck in his driveway, and you could see from his shorts that he had an amputated leg. Kelly was not shy. She marched across our adjacent yards, approached the new neighbor, and loudly asked, "Where is your leg?" The friendly neighbor put down the box he was carrying and turned to address her. He responded with a big smile, "I left it at home."

Much to my chagrin, she squatted down to get a closer look at his tan prosthetic. He recognized that Kelly could not grasp that he was joking, so he patted his leg with his hand and said, "This *is* my leg." Kelly responded, "Okay," and turned around to return across the yard and back to our house. I waved from my driveway, and he waved back. Then, as she walked away, he said with a smile, "Anytime you have questions, just let me know."

On a dime, she turned around, returned to him, and asked more questions. He answered questions like, "Why does your leg look like that?" and "Where is your other shoe?" I walked over to them as quickly as I could, interrupted her next question, introduced us, and welcomed him to the neighborhood.

Her curiosity and sociability began to diminish for Kelly.

After a few years in school, Kelly's confident approach to people transformed drastically. She regularly displayed self-doubt in her actions or called herself derogatory names like "Dummy" or "Stupid."

For example, we were in the grocery store checkout lane, and the assistant asked how our day was. As usual, Kelly started going through her entire day. "I got up late, but I still had waffles, and I sat next to Jeremy on the bus, but then he moved when Josh got on…." I watched the checker, who was trying to be polite and not interrupt her, finally say, "Jeez, that was a lot of information," as he handed us our receipt. I saw Kelly's face grow a look of concern.

When we got to the car, Kelly asked me if the checker thought she was just "stupid." I explained that sometimes, when people ask how you are doing, they don't want to know, and even if you're not doing well, it's polite to respond "fine" to people you don't know. I could tell this didn't make sense to her, as she remained focused on being perceived as "stupid" by the checker for her answer.

I wish I had paid more attention to her decrease in curiosity and had not brushed it aside as "just part of growing up" or accepted this change in her as something temporary that she would "grow out of,"thinking her adorable social and curious disposition would soon return.

She started out excited about school, but by the end of the first year, I had to encourage her to go. She said she had no friends, that the teacher didn't think she was trying hard, and that kids in class laughed at her when it was her time to read aloud.

I noticed that on her first report card at the beginning of the year, her teacher mentioned that Kelly did not listen attentively, but I figured this was just part of adjusting to the school's expectations. By the time I received her final report card at the end of the year, the teacher was praising Kelly for "recognizing her letters" and getting positive marks for knowing her sounds and sight words—all of which are requirements for passing to the next grade. Looking back, I realize she didn't recognize her letters, and I can't help but wonder why the teacher wanted to move her on to the next grade.

As they say, hindsight is 20/20. I sure wish I had paid more attention to Kelly's socialization patterns after starting public school, including her ability to make friends in her school surroundings. For example, I noticed during the days when I drove her to school that she consistently followed a direct path from car to building without acknowledging the waves from teachers who greeted her. I interpreted her seemingly focused and brisk behavior at the time as a young girl, knowing where she was supposed to go and getting there efficiently.

Later, I realized that she struggled with social skills, which contributed to her being incredibly misunderstood, isolated, and lonely. I thought it was odd that she did not talk about other children in her class.

Her frustration was not only related to social isolation but also to her inability to understand school assignments. After school, she spent at least an hour every weeknight trying to complete the homework assignments. Many nights, she worked for three hours on homework. She did not know where to start and wasn't sure what to do, and when I helped, it just made things worse.

I wish I had connected with her teacher sooner and shared her struggle with homework. Instead, I encouraged her to concentrate, listen, and try harder. I would do one problem, show her each step, and then ask her to do the next. She just stared at me, and I couldn't figure out why she wasn't doing the work, especially after she said she understood.

Was she being lazy? Didn't she care?

Why could she sit and take a toy apart for an hour but couldn't concentrate and finish reading or math?

She did homework before dinner, after dinner, and after bath time, but she still didn't finish it. Yet she was great at puzzles, and her ability to articulate and speak intelligently resulted in her vocabulary being off the charts!

RESEARCH INFORMATION:

Childhood Signs:
Several specific signs and behaviors may provide clues that a child has a neurodivergent learning style.

Children with neurodivergent learning styles often have difficulty with social interactions. Some may come across as naïve or socially awkward, but this is because they struggle to interpret social cues, gauge the emotions of others, and absorb lessons from social experience.

When they want approval from others, they might misbehave or appear overly eager or needy. Kelly was a pleaser from the get-go—she often let the teacher assume that she was fully comprehending a subject simply to please the teacher, even though she was struggling to understand the subject.

Neurodivergent children may sometimes laugh inappropriately. This may happen when they misunderstand social cues and respond in unexpected ways. Laughing can also be a way of coping with intense emotions.[1] For example, a neurodivergent person may express and relieve their discomfort by laughing nervously when they feel uneasy.

For some people with neurodivergent disabilities, social situations can pose challenges or confusion.

For example, neurodivergent students may struggle to adjust their voice volume. Sometimes, they may speak too loudly or quietly for the context without realizing it. This could be seen as a sign of trying to dominate the conversation when they may be unaware of the social norms for voice volume. Kelly knows that when I say, "I'm right here," her volume is louder than needed for the person in front of her to hear.

Many times, children's expressions are misinterpreted as sarcastic or inappropriate. Kelly explained that she appreciates it when I point out the disconnect between her facial expressions and specific conversations so she can think about it. It helps her to keep her communications authentic.

The situation can have added complexity when bias or negative attitudes from peers add unwanted negative attention toward those with disabilities. Students with neurodivergent disabilities often struggle to make and keep friends.[2] Kelly learns differently, and that affects her reading and writing skills. Her struggles were noticed and commented on by her peers. She fell far behind when her school did not help, and she became discouraged and unhappy.

As a result of the inability to respond as expected in peer-to-peer communications, bullying is a significant problem, leaving neurodivergent children more likely to be bullied. Children tend to be hypervigilant about the presence of any difference and pick on it upon noticing that difference. Since the playground's inception, a mob mentality has dominated it, and especially for children who are neurodivergent, the mob is rarely on their side.

Concentrated bullying can have a devastating, disorienting, and long-lasting negative impact on a child's confidence and sense of worth throughout their whole upbringing. Peers may become uncomfortable with neurodivergent children because they may find it difficult to read social signs or because they may behave in ways that are not deemed appropriate or even disrespectful. This may cause others to mock the perceived awkward behavior, worsening the problem.

Children with neurodivergent learning styles may also experience anxiety from external sensory overloads, such as feeling isolated among peers or entering a crowded and noisy classroom with many decorations and distractions. These situations can make it hard for the neurodivergent learner to concentrate, which affects their ability to pay attention and absorb relevant information.

Many Myths and Misconceptions:
Myths and prejudices impact the social interactions neurodivergent learners frequently encounter.

Many myths and misconceptions about specific learning disabilities can make it challenging to provide neurodivergent learners with the help they need. According to the American Psychological Association[3], these inaccurate beliefs cause severe delays in supporting the neurodivergent learner and may include:

• Waiting for things to get better due to the belief that children with learning disabilities will grow out of it.

• Misconception that there is no value in spending time or money on children with learning disabilities as they have a below-average IQ.

• The myth that specific learning disabilities are difficult and expensive to diagnose.

• The incorrect belief that children with specific learning disabilities are easily lumped in with or mixed up with autism spectrum disorders or attention deficit disorders.

• Ignorant misjudgments that a child with specific learning disabilities cannot learn or has below-average intelligence.

Just as I had heard that ADHD was rarely present in girls, there are several myths around ADHD. These include that ADHD is not a medical condition, that children eventually grow out of the medical condition, or that if the child tires harder, they can overcome the condition. Once, it was thought that all children with the condition were hyperactive; however, Attention Deficit was renamed, purposely removing the automatic nomenclature of "hyperactive." Another myth is that ADHD is a learning disability. It is classified within the neurological disorder umbrella. However, people who have an attention disorder often do not have a specific learning disability.

Unfortunately, myths can lead to acts of discrimination for neurodivergent learners, especially within their school setting. They are often misunderstood as a result of these myths. For example, it is not uncommon for neurodivergent learners to ask many questions as they try to understand their neurotypical learning environment. Asking questions can often help to fill in the blanks, but it also may be seen as a nuisance when excessive. For the neurodivergent learner, processing new information may be a struggle; therefore, hearing it multiple times is helpful and often a reason for the many questions.

It is important to note that children with specific learning disabilities are often of average to above-average intelligence. According to the College of Allied Educators, due to the many misconceptions, myths, and lack of knowledge surrounding specific learning disabilities, many children go undiagnosed or misdiagnosed, leading them to underperform, fail, or drop out of school. [4] The National Center for Learning Disabilities (2021) reports that students with specific learning disabilities drop out of high school at nearly three times the rate of their neurotypical peers.

Therefore, it is essential to understand the conditions that identify one with a specific learning disability (i.e., dyslexia, dysgraphia, dyspraxia, and ADHD) so they can be recognized and supported in early classroom years for an optimal and equitable learning opportunity.

Equally, ADHD needs to be tested and recognized, as children can feel misunderstood by their classmates and teachers at school for behaviors related to ADHD.

Challenges in the Classroom:
Kids with specific learning disabilities face more challenges when the classroom does not have the resources to support their participation in the curriculum. They may struggle to keep up with their studies, appear not to behave appropriately, or lack a sense of belonging in the class. For the neurodivergent learner without support, the classroom is like stepping onto a fast-moving treadmill already running at full speed. Each day, the setting increases, and they feel less and less hopeful of ever catching up.

This feeling of a lack of ability to keep up, understand, and adjust to their surrounding social situation results in exhaustion and sometimes triggers a fight/flight response. A neurodivergent individual may walk away as a coping mechanism for excessive sensory or heightened anxiety levels. Leaving without notice could be seen as rude, giving up, or demonstrating fear. This circumstance challenges the teacher and the student to succeed in the "regular" or neurotypical school setting.

REFERENCES:

[1] Jared C. Pistoia, ND. 2022. "Humor as a Coping Mechanism." Psych Central. June 28, 2022. https://

psychcentral.com/lib/humor-as-weapon-shield-and-psychological-salve#why-we-use-humor.

[2] Juliann Garey and Cynthia Martin, PsyD. 2023. "How Schools Can Support Neurodiverse Students." Child Mind Institute. August 23, 2023. https://childmind.org/article/how-schools-can-support-neurodiverse-students

[3] Dana S. Dunn, PhD. "Understanding Ableism and Negative Reactions to Disability." Https://Www.Apa.Org. https://www.apa.org/ed/precollege/psychology-teacher-network/introductory-psychology/ableism-negative-reactions-disability

[4] CAE. 2023. "What Is Specific Learning Disability (SLD)?" College of Allied Educators. January 17, 2023. https://cae.edu.sg/what-is-specific-learning-disability-sld

ACTION ITEMS:

1. Visit and audit your child's class. Is your child included in the lessons? Do they understand the directions and have the necessary resources for the in-class assignments? Visit our website at neuro-navigation.com to download our class audit tool.

2. Find who has these roles in your child's school and ask the assistant for their email address: school psychologist, school counselor, school assistant principal, school principal, superintendent, and school district.

3. Write a letter to include all the above school members, sharing your observations from the audit and your child's observations in treatment from peers. Ask for their suggestions to address the concerns within a specific timeframe.

YOUR NEURODIVERSITY ENABLES YOU TO GROW THROUGH WHAT YOU GO THROUGH.

CHAPTER 3

MISLABELED: SPECIFIC LEARNING DISABILITIES IN SPECIAL EDUCATION

I began to dread when school started back up, as each new year seemed to be worse than the last.

This year, I took a different bus to the same school. I rode a short yellow bus that I had to walk down the block to catch. There was something very different about this bus and the few kids who rode it with me. I didn't talk to any of them, but they seemed nice.

When the short bus arrived at school, I got off but did not know where to go, so I followed a kid I had recognized from my class the year before. We walked into a big classroom with lots of desks. Like the previous classroom, this room was bright and colorful, with many pictures, signs, and symbols on the walls. The windows flooded the room with bright outside light, while the ceiling lights gave everything in the classroom a harsh white glow.

I walked to the window and looked outside. There was the playground.

It was vibrant in color, and I could not wait to try out the swings, slides, and rock-climbing walls. I had often walked by the rock climbing wall with my mom, and

I could hear the kids cheering on the climbers. I was finally old enough to be out there!

But as I thought about recess time, a woman grabbed my shoulder and said, "You're in the wrong class!"

Apparently, I was supposed to be in a room down the other hall. A teacher I had not seen before walked me to my new room, and the teacher inside came to meet us in the doorway. The two teachers talked to me and said I would have to follow directions if I did not want privileges taken away. I had no idea what that meant, but I knew it was not good by the seriousness on their face when they said it. The stern tone scared me. I walked into the classroom, and the teacher pointed to a desk in the back, telling me to "sit."

As I sat down, the teacher started talking to everyone and walked to the front of the class. I noticed there was gum under my desk, and I went under to see it. I heard the teacher say, "Kelly! Get back in your seat." I tried to tell her about the gum, but she did not want me to interrupt her talking. I sat there as quietly as I could until she finally said we would each get a book. She called my name and the name of another person and asked us to hand out books, paper, and pencils. I could not remember all of those directions. So, I went to the large pile of books she pointed to on her desk, grabbed one, and sat down. The teacher must not have been happy with me as she told me I was being rude, taking one book instead of handing it out to others, and some of the kids in the class laughed.

After two children handed out books, paper, and pencils, the teacher told us to read pages one to three and use our pencils and paper to answer the questions on the board. I raised my hand for help, but the teacher repeated the instructions and said, "Get to work; time is almost up."

Before I knew it, the teacher said, "Times up," and then called on the person in front of me to read the first question and their answer. It wasn't until she answered the question that I realized the book was about sharks. The only pictures I could find were of clownfish, turtles, and sea urchins. The question asked was to identify the giant shark. The kid got it right, and I could tell the teacher was pleased. She kept going through all the kids in each row and finally got to me and asked me to read my question and my answer.

Um... The entire room shrank around me.

"I don't know," I said.

She walked to my desk, turned the page in my book, and pointed at several things on the page, saying,

"Read this, please,".

I tried, but I did not get any of the words right. I heard some kids laugh, so I started laughing, too. The teacher skipped past me and asked the next kid to read their question and answer. The person behind me read the question and the correct answer about how many different kinds of sharks were on the page. It was the first of many times I was embarrassed, laughed at, and skipped.

At least there was recess to look forward to...sometimes. Most days, I was late to recess because I needed to finish my classroom work. When I got to the playground, I would ask others if they wanted to play, but the kids were already doing something. So, most days on the playground, I just collected rocks or watched the cars drive by until the bell went off and it was time to go back inside. I started to feel very lonely at school.

My school-day loneliness intensified in fourth grade when, every day, a teacher assistant came and got me from my classroom and took me to an outside portable building.

My school had four outside portables that were converted from fifth-wheel trailers into miniature classrooms. Inside each was a similar setup to the building classrooms, with a teacher's desk, student chairs, and a whiteboard—the whiteboard in the portable was super tiny compared to the giant one in the building classroom. Another big difference was that there were no windows in the portables, just noisy fans. The portable I attended was for my special lessons, and sometimes, we had the PE teacher during this time. We knew this because he said he usually taught PE and was helping until the school could hire more teachers.

My dark brown classroom portable included students of different grades and some with various needs. For example, one kid had bubble-shaped glasses, a big smile, and a hearing aid. On most days, we had the same kids in our portable, but sometimes, when a regular kid was in trouble, our portable was his timeout space until his mom came to get him.

When reading or testing time happened in my regular classroom, I would get sent to the portable. At the time, I didn't realize this was a special education classroom, but I could tell this portable classroom was not for most kids. It was for kids like me who were different, not normal. Each day, in the portable, I sat next to Adrian, a boy two grades bigger than me. In the portable, we each sat at separate desks with headphones on behind trifold plastic desk shields that we could not see around so we would not be distracted by our surroundings. Most days, I was given a book and told to practice reading it. It was the same book I had in class, so I usually looked through it until the time was up and someone took me back to the regular classroom. Sometimes, an older kid from the regular classroom would come to get us and take us back; other times, I went alone.

I realized that I was taken to the portables because I slowed down the teacher in my regular classroom. She would say, "Raise your hand if you have questions," I remember my hand going to sleep because it was in the air for so long, but she did not come to my desk or call on me. She just waited until it was time for me to be taken to the portable. I stopped raising my hand, hoping to stay in the regular classroom, but I still had to go to the portable.

I didn't feel like I belonged in the portable, but I guess I didn't belong in my regular classroom, either.

The only good thing about the portable was missing "group time" with the kids in my regular classroom. Sometimes, when the teacher was absent and the PE teacher wasn't available, I did not go to the portable. These days, I stayed in my regular classroom and joined regular kids in group activities. I dreaded group time because I never felt like I understood what we were doing, and one time, I heard a boy in my group say he did not want me in his group. This was the same kid who would call me a "tard" or "loser" on the playground. When I told the playground teacher he was calling me names, she said to avoid him. Others called me names, too, so I tried not to listen to them and stay away. It's not easy to stay away from other kids while at school.

I had many confusing days in school. Interacting with peers never seemed to go well, and I had trouble figuring out exactly why or what went wrong.

One day a girl in my regular classroom, Sarah, announced that everyone in the class was invited to her birthday party. The teacher gave each student a card with Sarah's birthday information. I brought home the invitation and showed it to my mom. I did not know Sarah, but this was exciting—a birthday party at the park!

My mom and I wrapped the Tamagotchi gift we got for Sarah and went to the park together for the birthday party. My mom said hello, then goodbye to some other moms, and I was told to put the gift on a picnic table and join the kids in the inflatable jumping castle.

When I climbed into the bouncing house, I realized I still had the present and heard someone say, "Why is SHE here?"

The same kid made fun of me during a game with rules I did not understand.

I am not sure what I did—I was nine years old, after all—but two moms at the party were upset with me for some reason, and they asked me to sit at a different picnic table away from the group until my mom came back to pick me up.

I was told to go elsewhere, even at my classmate's birthday party. It took everything I had not to cry in front of everyone while watching them play birthday games from the table. I went under the picnic table so I couldn't be seen.

It felt like forever, but I was so glad when my mom's car came around the corner. I ran to the car, started crying, and told her, "Let's go home!" I never went to another birthday party.

MOM'S PERSPECTIVE:

Kelly was placed in the "Special Education" system with little understanding of what it meant. For some reason, I understood it to be temporary until she "caught up." That's how it was described to me during a parent-teacher conference, anyway. It sounded like a good plan. My understanding was that she would get the extra help she needed. I didn't ask too many questions. They knew better than I did, I figured. It wasn't until a surprise visit that I discovered the Special Education room was a por-table—outside the main school building. The school had four portables; at least one was designated for children pulled from their regular assigned classrooms.

The teachers in her assigned portable were not always qualified to teach special education. One genuinely excellent teacher told me he was a PE teacher who was only asked to fill in on certain occasions. In one semester, he was in the portable for several weeks. Although it was needed, it was evident that personalized learning attention per student did not increase in special education.

The decision to move Kelly from a regular classroom to special education had consequences—a reality for any student transitioning to a different classroom setting. In hindsight, I would have been more proactive in understanding that school decision. I wish I had asked questions and learned about Kelly's needs and how the school's offerings would meet each learning need. Some schools' special education programs may be precisely what your child needs…or not. And you really won't know until your child shifts to the new setting. Having gone through it now, I recommend having a plan to measure the success before they transition and looking for the clues—their socialization patterns, learning ability, and self-confidence to identify a smooth transition. The progress, or lack thereof, will often come through observation. And unless you're tuned in to your child's mood and behavioral changes, you might not recognize the situation for what it is. The right environment will help your child feel included instead of excluded and will put them in positions to grow, learn, progress, and feel a sense of belonging.

RESEARCH INFORMATION:

Setting Things Up for Success:
According to The Learning Scientists, the special education system may not be suitable for the neurodivergent learner.[1] They suggest that neurodivergent learners often have unique needs that are not met by traditional special education programs and that addressing these unique needs can be a multipronged approach that includes one or more of the following:

- **Create an Inclusive Environment:** Teachers who create an inclusive environment that considers each student's unique needs will find fewer disruptive behaviors. This can be achieved using various teaching methods and materials catering to different learning styles.

- **Provide Accommodations:** Providing accommodations such as extra time on tests or assignments, preferential seating arrangements, and assistive technology can help neurodivergent students find their success in the classroom.

- **Collaborate with Parents:** Teachers who collaborate with parents to understand the child's unique needs and work with school resources to develop strategies that support each learner will contribute to the student's ongoing success.

- **Be Flexible:** Teachers who are flexible in their approach to teaching and willing to adapt their methods to meet their students' needs will have students who experience more significant outcomes.

- **Encourage Self-Advocacy:** Encouraging self-advocacy can help neurodivergent students develop self-awareness and self-confidence. Teachers can help students express their needs and preferences so they can act on them.

The Importance of Accommodations:
Individuals with neurodivergence can face significant challenges in an educational environment where accommodations are not made for their condition. Some of these challenges include:

- Difficulty retaining information presented only by auditory methods

- Struggling to process written information

- Problems with processing multisensory information presented simultaneously

- Difficulty intaking lecture information while simultaneously documenting notes

As a result, it is crucial to identify each student's learning style to tailor a successful approach when delivering new information. Otherwise, overwhelmed learners lose their ability to learn successfully.

It is important not to assume but to identify each student's learning style. Students often mask their differences by suppressing natural neurodivergent responses and knowledge and by imitating "neurotypical behaviors" to avoid adverse reactions from others. Kelly mastered blending in to avoid being called upon in her classroom. According to a study by Pearson and Rose (2021), masking differences inhibits learning and can lead to exhaustion and burnout, disconnection from one's identity, and psychological distress.[2] It's imperative that masking behavior is recognized and that support is provided for a positive correction in behavior and an opportunity for the student to learn and build on the lessons being taught.

Neurodivergent Accommodations in the Classroom:
It's important to provide alternatives and choices throughout classroom activities to create learning environments that support a wide range of neurotypes. One example is that teachers can use various strategies, such as flipped classrooms or project-based learning, which are often effective for neurodivergent students.[3]

Other helpful strategies for neurodivergent learners include breaking projects down into smaller steps, focusing on short-term goals, taking short breaks to help kids release energy, minimizing distractions, simplifying tasks and instructions, keeping feedback positive, and matching homework demands to a child's capacity. These techniques should also be practiced at home to create consistency and increase the opportunity to learn.

By creating these safe and inclusive classroom environments that accommodate the needs of all students, teachers help foster a greater understanding and positive attitudes toward neurodiversity among their students.

REFERENCES:

[1] The Learning Scientists. 2021. "Digest #153: Neurodiversity in Education — The Learning Scientists." The Learning Scientists. October 12, 2021. https://www.learningscientists.org/blog/2021/6/25/digest-153.

[2] Amy Pearson and Kieran Rose. 2021. "A Conceptual Analysis of Autistic Masking: Understanding the Narrative of Stigma and the Illusion of Choice." Autism in Adulthood 3 (1): 52—60. https://doi.org/10.1089/aut.2020.0043

[3] Carrie Bredow and Patricia Roehling. 2021. "Flipped Learning: What Is It, and When Is It Effective?" Brookings, September 28, 2021. https://www.brookings.edu/articles/flipped-learning-what-is-it-and-when-is-it-effective

ACTION ITEMS:

1. Ask specifically for the school to conduct an audit identifying your child's reading comprehension, processing, and knowledge retention of the subject taught in the classroom.

2. Research and create positive study methods (note taking, content comprehension, etc.) and a positive homework environment (quiet space, regular breaks, minimal distractions, etc.) specific to your child's needs. Share what works at home with the teachers and ask if they can provide something similar in their classroom experience.

3. Speak with your child, identify the specific challenges within the school system they encounter daily, and work together on a plan to address them.

WHILE UNIQUE, YOU ARE NORMAL. WHILE ISOLATED, YOU ARE NOT ALONE.

CHAPTER 4

SILENT STRUGGLES: NAVIGATING LEARNING INEQUITIES AND BULLYING

Adrian was a jerk.

He always went first, argued when he got the answer wrong, and once got so upset that he knocked over a chair in the portable. One time, when the teacher was out, I saw him take the teacher's answers from their book and claim they were his. I didn't say anything because I understood why he did it.

I was never scared of Adrian because I could feel he wasn't angry—he was incredibly frustrated, which is different. I know how it feels when you are so frustrated because no one around you understands—and sometimes you don't understand either. For example, nobody understood when I tried to describe being allergic to paper. I felt like I had lizard-dry skin, and the paper edge dragged on every scale, pulling it slightly backward and making my whole body itch. Or when an adult looked at me like I was stupid and said, "Does that make sense?" Or worse, when they told me I wasn't trying hard enough because I could not read the symbols that kept flashing and float-ing on the page. Many letters looked like each other; it was hard to tell them apart. Sometimes, it felt like I was trying to read a plate of spaghetti, and with the fluorescent lights, the harder I stared, the more flashing happened, like being in a dark room with a strobe light. It was hard to explain, and it was much easier to say I couldn't or didn't want to do the task.

I felt like Adrian was a jerk because he always acted like he knew more than me. Even though he was a jerk, I still had to spend a lot of time at school paired with him—from third grade until we both left elementary school. I think we were paired together so much because we were most alike compared to the other kids in the special education portable class.

Every morning after the pledge of allegiance, each portable kid was gathered from the regular classrooms to spend most of the day in the special education portable. Even though Adrian was two grades older than me, we had the same reading and math lessons and the same workbooks. Sometimes, the teacher would put us in the corner of the portable, do a lesson with us, and then let us work together on the same lesson in our workbooks.

Because of the portable, Adrian and I spent time together; other kids were in the portable classroom but were usually not there for most of the day like us.

I remember being on the playground with Adrian one day after lunch. We noticed a teacher was sitting in a chair, handing out ice cream cups from a big cooler in front of her. Adrian said the ice cream was free if you could answer her question. He said it was too hard, so he didn't want to try.

I decided to stand in line to try and get an ice cream cup. I stood in the back of the line and saw one by one how the line got shorter as each kid in the front of the line would say a number, get ice cream, and leave the line. As I got closer, I noticed a kid in front said,

"Two." They got an ice cream cup and left the line. The next kid in line said, "Four," and he got an ice cream cup and left the line. The kid before me said, "Six," and got an ice cream cup and left the line. I stood there, finally at the front. The teacher looked at me and asked, "What's the next number?" I stood there. I heard the kids behind me say different numbers. "Six," I whispered to the lady handing out the ice cream. She said no, that's not the correct answer; try again. I suddenly felt all the noise on the playground amplify so loud I could not think. I said, "I don't know," and stood there feeling paralyzed but wanting to run away. She said, "Good try," and gave me an ice cream cup. As I left the line with my cup of ice cream, I heard the next person in line say, "Hey, no fair! She cheated!"

I was embarrassed and did not understand how each kid knew the different numbers to get their ice cream cup. Adrian did not even try. He and I leaned against the corner of the building and ate my ice cream together as we watched the kids eating their cups from afar.

Even if Adrian could be a jerk, I liked some things about him. He was the only one who seemed to understand how hard school was. Plus, he was the only kid willing to read with me.

Each month, I would get a new magazine in my mailbox at home. My favorites were the *National Geographic Kids* and *Highlights for Children* magazines. After doing the mazes, I would bring my Highlights magazines to class and let Adrian read the stories. Adrian always read aloud, so I also got to hear the story.

Many times, when the teacher left the portable or when we had reading/quiet time, I would pull out the magazine I had snuck into school, and Adrian and I would read it. We worked on the rest of the puzzles together, but sometimes, he would get frustrated and scribble over the entire page. I could not complain to the teacher because I was not supposed to have the magazine at school. The truth is, I wish I knew how to read so I didn't need Adrian to help me.

I did not know when my reading powers would start. I remember when I was in the regular class, early on, and we had circle time—the teacher would sit in a chair, and all the students would sit at her feet on a big green carpet. The teacher held up a card and asked someone to sound out the word. Everyone raised their hand, hoping to be selected to answer her question. The teacher called on someone else, and they said, "Two-mar-Row." The teacher said, "Great job!" and then showed the next card and asked who could sound it out. She picked on one of the kids in front, who was bouncing up and down.

The student answered correctly, and I heard the teacher say with excitement, "That's correct!"

The teacher was so happy when we got the answer right. She kept reading cards and selecting a raised hand. But during this excitement, I noticed that the carpet was itchy on the back of my legs, so I got up on my knees, but that didn't help. So I flopped over on my back and tried to get more comfortable. When I looked up, I saw the ceiling lights pulsating. I turned my head away from the lights and noticed the untied shoe on the person next to me. My mind started to race with different thoughts. I wondered if they knew how to tie shoes or if they could teach me how to tie shoes. My shoes did not need to be tied because I used Velcro. I started to open and close my Velcro shoes. I heard "Kelly….," "Kelly….," "KELLY"! I came out of my mental zone and heard the teacher calling my name. I responded with my usual answer, "I don't know," and everyone laughed. I laughed, too. The teacher said, "It's desk time. Everyone has returned to their desk, please return to yours." I was surprised to realize that I was the only one still on the green carpet.

I remember one of the things the teacher said I had to do before the end of one school year was done was to recite my name, birthday, address, and phone number. Every Friday in this class, we had a test about this, and I failed it every time. I didn't understand the meaning behind these things, where to get them, how to memorize them, or why they were important.

My teacher tried to help me, so on test day, she would ask us to come to the front and recite our information. By the end of that school year, I could say, "KellyVanZant1120," and she would say, "That's fine." I was relieved to finish that class and move to the next grade.

While I knew I couldn't do what the other kids were doing, I was happy to be done with the class and hoped that things would be easier next year.

MOM'S PERSPECTIVE:

I realized Kelly was having bad days and was stressed, but I did not know how to help. She would regularly come home exhausted. She wanted to drop items at the front door, lie on the closest couch, and not get up. At first, I insisted on her putting everything away, washing her hands, and helping with a chore or two as I prepared a snack for her to eat while working on homework. This is how I was raised. But it did not take me long to see that she was genuinely out of energy.

One of the mistakes I made was trying to recreate what I was exposed to as a child, even if it was for the best intentions. When I finally realized she was independent and wired quite differently from me, I started to listen and make the necessary adjustments to make our home better for both of us.

At the beginning of elementary school, I helped Kelly with her homework. After about two hours of trying, both of us were discouraged. I wrote the answers for her and explained how I got them. My attempts to teach her were different from what she saw in class, and this, unfortunately, added confusion to understanding the problem-solving method. While I am sure her teachers realized the work she turned in was someone else answering her homework sheets, they never mentioned it.

Time spent doing homework was such a negative experience for both of us. She would sit at the kitchen table but could not focus. I would stop what I was doing and sit with her to keep her focused. I would read one of the homework problems, and she would have no idea how to answer a question related to the problem I had just read. I would give a hint, and she would start fidgeting by picking at the paint on the pencil, or she would notice something happening out the window. "PAY ATTENTION!" I would surprise us both when I blurted out my words with emotions of frustration. All I could think about was the tasks I needed to get done but could not because she was not taking this homework seriously.

At a parent-teacher conference, I asked her teacher why there was so much homework. The teacher seemed surprised and asked how long it took to do homework each night. When I shared that it took around two hours most school nights, she gasped and responded that the homework assignments were 15 to 30 minutes maximum! Then, the teacher explained that they did the same questions in the classroom, so it was mostly a review. After the parent-teacher meeting, when I mentioned this to Kelly, she responded that she had never seen the schoolwork or didn't recall how to do it, saying the teacher went too fast. The teacher offered to send written instructions home. This didn't make much of a difference in Kelly's success in understanding or getting her homework completed.

One day, I decided to drop into her school, surprise her, and take her to lunch for fun. The school welcomed me when I checked in at the front desk and pointed me to the classroom. When I walked into her classroom, the teacher instructed me to go to the portable. When I entered the brown portable, I was horrified to discover that Kelly was completely segregated in a corner. She sat at a desk facing the corner, with headphones on and a tall white plastic "blinder" attached to the edge of her desk to prevent her from looking outward. The teacher smiled, greeted me, and shared that lunch was not for another 30 minutes; however, it would be OK to take Kelly early. Kelly was already turned around and looking at us but turned back when the teacher approached her. The teacher tapped Kelly on the shoulder, and she was ecstatic to hear she could leave with me! She started walking toward the exit before I could even say hello. As we left the portable, I noticed the other students were focused on different open books or papers on their desks.

I asked the teacher about Kelly's seating arrangement at the next teacher-parent conference. She explained that they tried multiple times to get Kelly to sit still at her desk and pay attention, and this setup had the best result. The teacher also shared that Kelly often would lose her privileges—helping with different tasks in the classroom (known as the Teacher's Helper) and going outside for recess—for not following directions. She continued by saying that Kelly was a very bright child, but she did not apply herself. Kelly did not pay attention, and she gave up too quickly. She noted that Kelly talked too much in class and needed to listen to the directions so she could follow through. This was not new to me, as I heard this at every teacher-parent conference. It was the same rhetoric: teachers expecting Kelly to conform and produce results.

The report cards consistently said the same things— she was "falling behind," she needed to attend summer school, and she needed to try harder at home to catch up. This encouraged me to look outside for help. I signed her up for private tutoring at Kumon and then Sylvan Learning. She went every Saturday, Sunday, and even during summer while attending summer school programs. Yet, year after year, she passed to the next classroom with the same failing grades and written notices of concern about her not applying herself.

One teacher during a third-grade school event mentioned that maybe she was "dyslexic" but then said, "It's too early to know for sure…time will tell." I did not know what to do with that information.

RESEARCH INFORMATION:

Learning Style:
Comprehending each individual's unique learning styles and preferences is crucial, particularly for neurodivergent learners. Learning styles determine how best they can pick up new abilities, expand their knowledge, and

retain information. More often than not, their particular learning style is the only format in which the material can be grasped by the neurodivergent learner, making it more than just a preference. Visual and hands-on learning are common among neurodivergent learners every day. To be sure, every individual must have the chance to find what best suits their needs. While several models explain learning preferences, VARK—an acronym for visual, auditory, reading/writing, and kinesthetic—is widespread.[1]

To utilize the appropriate learning styles, it is critical to understand them. A visual learner processes knowledge that is best presented visually, such as through graphs, photographs, diagrams, or even by sketching out concepts. Auditory learners will discover that hearing the material read aloud or broken down into manageable chunks helps them concentrate on the subject matter and reduces distractions while using skills like when they are reading the material. Reading aloud and writing down the words representing the learning content can be a physical connection to a reading/writing learning style, that helps the learner retain and comprehend the information more thoroughly.

Additionally, a kinesthetic learner will value experiential learning opportunities involving other senses (touch, smell, sight, taste, etc.) that enhance comprehension of the information.

While having many learning styles is not unusual, it is more typical to have a preferred type that optimizes one's capacity to assimilate and understand new information.

It's also typical for learning preferences to shift as a person gets older. Thus, it's a good idea to periodically reassess learning style preferences to determine which approaches work best.

Finally, each neurodivergent person can use their abilities to understand the material when it is taught in their preferred learning style.

Teaching Strategies:

Schools' learning environments should include all learners—including those with disabilities you cannot see—and should be a North Star for learning and development strategies. Here are some methods that have been effective for Kelly, a neurodivergent learner with specific learning disabilities (dyslexia, dysgraphia, dyscalculia) and ADHD.

- **Avoid Big Blocks of Text**: Neurodiverse people may find it harder to process large blocks of text. Breaking down the content into smaller chunks and using fonts designed explicitly for neurodivergent students (i.e., Dyslexia font) may be helpful.

- **Use Visual Aids**: Visual aids such as diagrams, charts, and images can help neurodiverse learners understand complex concepts better. Kelly found that transparent overlay (i.e., rose-colored) allowed the letters to be seen more clearly and not "float" on the page.

- **Provide Multiple Learning Options**: Providing multiple learning options can help neurodiverse learners engage with comprehending and retaining the content.

- **Remove the Distractions**: Pay attention to what is causing the barriers to learning. This might be the clock ticking in the background, feeling overwhelmed by the total work volume, or the teaching material (e.g., avoid scratchy paper or uncomfortable writing instruments).

- **Be Patient:** Neurodivergent learners may need more time to process information than neurotypical learners. Therefore, it is essential to be patient and allow them to work at their own pace while checking in regularly to provide support and encouragement.

- **Encourage Collaboration:** Collaboration among learners can help neurodivergent learners feel more comfortable in the learning environment. It also helps them develop social skills that are essential for success in life.

- **Provide Accommodations:** Providing accommodations such as extra time on tests or reducing assignment repetition can help neurodivergent learners succeed in the classroom.

- **Create a Safe Learning Environment:** Creating a safe learning environment where neurodivergent learners feel comfortable asking questions and seeking help is essential for their success and acceptance of diversity in our communities.

Specific Learning Disability Teaching Strategies:
Here are some specific strategies that can be used in the classroom for neurodivergent students who have specific learning disabilities in a neurotypical classroom[2]:

- **Create an Inclusive Learning Environment:** The teacher's words and attitude can help develop a welcoming environment for students. Encourage the neurodivergent learner to ask questions and participate in class discussions. Ensure equity in learning the lesson and that students feel valued and respected throughout the learning process.

- **Familiarize Yourself with Students' Unique Rhythms:** Students with learning disabilities may have different learning styles and rhythms than others. Teachers should take the time to get to know each student and their individual needs.

- **Intentional Classroom Seating:** Seating arrangements can significantly impact student learning. Consider your students with learning disabilities seating placement within the classroom and ensure they are near the front, away from distractions, and in a quiet area.

- **Practice Consistency:** Consistency is critical when working with students with learning disabilities. Teachers must establish and stick to daily routines, using the same language and procedures.

- **Encourage Social Interactions:** Social interactions can be challenging for students with learning disabilities. Encourage group work and pair students together for activities. Supervise these as needed and provide positive criticism for social growth.

- **Visual Aids and Stimuli:** Visual aids can be helpful for all learners but are essential for students with learning disabilities. Ensure your student's classroom uses diagrams, charts, and other visual aids to help explain concepts.

- **Flexible and Informed:** New techniques and technologies are constantly being developed to help students with learning disabilities.

Help your teacher stay current on the latest research and resources and encourage them to try novel approaches.

Attention Deficit Teaching Strategies:
These strategies are not exhaustive but can be used as a starting point to help support students with specific learning disabilities in a neurotypical classroom. Here are some strategies that can help attention deficit (ADHD) students succeed in a neurotypical classroom: [3]

- **Behavioral Classroom Management:** This approach encourages positive behavior in the classroom through a reward system or a daily report card and discourages negative behavior. This teacher-led approach has been shown to influence student behavior constructively, increasing academic engagement.

- **Organizational Training:** This strategy teaches children time management, planning skills, and ways to organize school materials to optimize student learning and reduce distractions.

- **Short-Term Goals:** Focusing on short-term goals can help students with ADHD stay motivated and engaged in their work.

- **Breaking Projects Down into Smaller Steps:** Breaking down projects into smaller steps can help students with ADHD feel less overwhelmed and more capable of completing their work.

- **Rewarding Good Behavior and Work:** This helps to reinforce and define positive socialization skills and goes a long way toward supporting their success.

- **Taking Short Breaks to Help Kids Release Energy:** Short breaks can help students with ADHD release energy and refocus on their work.

It is essential to find out if your student's school offers ADHD treatments such as behavioral classroom management or organizational training, special education ADHD services, or accommodations to lessen the effect of ADHD on learning. It's recommended that you also bring in all the experts and keep them connected on the efforts being implemented. This means talking to your child's healthcare providers and teachers about working together to support the child.

Recognizing strengths is also impactful for inclusion. Once the barriers to literacy are removed or minimized, your child's strengths can be revealed. This may include recognizing their artistic side, the child's creative mind, the ability to be empathic toward others, patience in the process, and articulating their needs. Identifying, promoting, and celebrating strengths is meaningful in developing self-confidence and self-worth.

REFERENCES:

[1] VARK Learn Limited. 2024. "VARK Learning Styles." VARK - Helping You Learn Better. March 1, 2024. https://vark-learn.com

[2] *UNESCO*. 2023. "The Right to Quality Education for Learners With Disabilities: What Makes a Learning Environment Inclusive?" April 20, 2023. https://www.unesco.org/en/articles/right-quality-education-learners-disabilities-what-makes-learning-environment-inclusive

[3] Gretchen Vierstra, MA. 2023. "8 ADHD Teaching Strategies." Understood. October 5, 2023. https://www.understood.org/en/articles/adhd-teaching-strategies

ACTION ITEMS:

1. Ask the teacher what strategies are currently being tried to support your child's learning efforts. Feel free to show them the ones listed in this chapter!

2. Explore the options of specialized programs for neurodivergent students within your community.

3. Document, document, document! Keep any/all progress letters your child receives. Document how much time/effort goes into homework. Document your child's experience of school as they share it with you.

YOU CAN RECOGNIZE, ACQUIRE, AND IMPLEMENT THE TOOLS NEEDED FOR LEARNING EQUITY OPPORTUNITIES!

CHAPTER 5

FROM FEAR TO HOPE: RECEIVING A DIAGNOSIS AND ACCOMMODATIONS

Mom says we are going on a trip. I am excited! We always go on fun adventures. We once visited a tiny rainforest and stayed at a cabin on the beach.

But during the car ride, she explained that this trip was different and we were headed to see a particular doctor. This made me nervous.

"Do I have to get shots?" Mom assures me that there are no shots at this doctor's office. We drive all morning, and she pulls the car into an empty parking lot next to a big gray-brick building.

Hmmm.

We leave the car and walk toward the building, holding hands. Something is different about Mom, as she seems more serious than usual. We enter the building and a smiling lady named Carol greets us.

"We were expecting you," says Carol with a big smile. "Please fill out this paperwork." She gives my mom a clipboard and paper. Mom and I sit in one of the chairs, and I ask if it is okay if I look at the fish tank. Before I get to the fish tank, a man opens a door next to Carol and calls my name. The man introduces himself as Dr. Carlaw.

My Mom and I followed him back through the door he came through, down a short hall, and into a well-lit spacious room painted dark purple but with no windows.

The purple room has books all the way up to the ceiling, just like a library. What caught my eye were all the different and exciting colored puzzle blocks and strange-looking toys on the bookshelves and, even more, on a small table in the corner. Dr. Carlaw tells me I can sit at the small table and investigate the items. I do this, and he and Mom go to another nearby, bigger table across the room and talk.

When Mom and Dr. Carlaw finish talking, she comes to the small table where I sit. Mom says she will be in the lobby and that I should listen closely to Dr. Carlaw's instructions. The truth is, I barely listened to what she was saying because I just wanted to get back to the puzzle in front of me. Mom leaves the purple room, and Dr. Carlaw helps me finish my puzzle.

Over the next several days, Dr. Carlaw and I worked on different puzzles, and he asked me lots of questions and then wrote down my answers. He is very patient when he waits for my answer; if I don't know, he doesn't seem upset. Sometimes, he and I walk down the hall into a different room resembling a science room. I do various tests in this smaller room at different "stations." For example, I put headphones on at one station and raise my hand as I watch a dot move around on a screen. At another station, I listen to a story and then tell Dr. Carlaw what the story was about, or I try to answer his questions about the story. Most of the tests are interesting because I've never done them before; some are even fun!

Mom takes me to Dr. Carlaw's office for three days, and he and I each day play different games, talk, and do "tests." But again, the tests are not like any tests I have at school. Some of the tests are fun, and others are confusing because I don't understand or can't remember their rules. When that happens, we skip those tests, and Dr. Carlaw gives me something else to do. We take snack breaks, but he mostly shows me new papers and worksheets with drawings and figures and asks me lots of questions. Once I answer all his questions on each paper, he says with a big smile that I have done an excellent job, and I get a reward of another break to play with the table toys.

At the end of each day, I return to the lobby and tell Mom all about the "assessments" I did with Dr. Carlaw. Mom smiles, and we leave the lobby and head to find some dinner.

After the third day of testing, he says we are finally done. I happily stay in the purple room at the small table while he goes to the lobby to bring my mom in to join us.

MOM'S PERSPECTIVE:

I was desperate. And I needed expert help. Fast!

As I drove to the Independent Education Evaluation center, the voice in my head said, "I know Kelly is smart and capable…the suggestion back in third grade that maybe she had dyslexia. That didn't make sense. No one in my family has dyslexia."

The voice in my head wondered if I could only prove that—if I could get a professional opinion that every-thing was okay with Kelly—she could move forward with learning in her school. For crying out loud, she was almost ten and couldn't recognize her first name, let alone write it.

Then, the voice in my head started to spiral into negative thoughts. Oh my god, she is the definition of being illiterate. Oh my god! How will she graduate? If she doesn't graduate, how will she get a job? How will she read an electric bill? She won't be able to get her driver's license, and she won't…

STOP! I told myself.

Deep breath…don't spiral. If the school can't figure out what to do, this doctor will surely be able to help. This is good; I'm doing this….I can't just keep waiting. She can't afford to continue to be sent to the next grade only to get further behind. My thoughts started spiraling again…It was the teachers who needed to try harder! Why wasn't the school taking this more seriously? The frantic dialog in my head stopped as I noticed we were here.

I double-checked the address and found a parking space near the front door. The address was correct. I got out of the car and walked around the front of it, meeting up with Kelly. We'd started walking toward the front door of the doctor's office when I felt Kelly grab my hand and look up at me, smiling. I smiled back. Maybe this specialized doctor could give us strategies to take back to the school so Kelly's teachers would be better at teaching her. I would not be surprised when he told me that it's not her; it's how they teach her.

I searched for hours online before finding Dr. Carlaw, a highly-rated neuropsychologist.

I called Dr. Carlaw's office over a month earlier. It had been a particularly difficult morning—I'd struggled for an hour with Kelly because she was, again, saying she didn't want to go back to school. I shared my story with the receptionist as we made an appointment for a three-day comprehensive education evaluation. She was comforting and reassuring, and I provided her with the first down payment.

The testing days were long and grueling. Kelly didn't seem to mind, but the long drive and extra days off of work were draining for me. I would bring Kelly in at 8 a.m., wait in the lobby until noon, take her to lunch, then bring her back, stay in the lobby again until 3 p.m., and drive three hours back home—to do it again the next day.

Kelly was missing school, but it was a last-ditch effort to find help. On the third day, when we returned from lunch, Kelly and I followed the doctor from his lobby to the back area. We went into a large office, and he asked Kelly if she would be interested in playing with the puzzle toys on the small table. She accepted his invitation and sat quietly for our conversation.

While Kelly focused her attention on playing in the corner, I sat on a couch, and the doctor pulled up a chair from his desk and sat across from me. He handed me a stack of papers, the results from the last three days, which were compiled into a lengthy report. Before reviewing the data, Dr. Carlaw asked me if I remembered why I wanted Kelly to be tested. I recounted to him that I needed him to give me a signed doctor's note to return to her teachers ...to prove that Kelly didn't have dyslexia. I don't have dyslexia in my family. Kelly wasn't dyslexic; she was struggling because of issues with the teaching methods. "Exactly," he said and continued, "So before we start, I want to say something that will likely surprise you." He paused, then continued, "To help Kelly, you must first get over yourself." His comment stunned me!

He told me Kelly is very different from me; she views, comprehends, and processes the world differently. He asked me to be open-minded as he explained that Kelly has neurological disorders that include being dyslexic and, therefore, she is not a neurotypical learner.

Huh? But she looked identical to me when I was her age, and I never had this problem.

He continued with a gentle smile across his face, "Kelly is a clever girl. She has the potential to read, write, and even go to college if she wants, but," he paused again, "she has specific learning disabilities, and she has an attention deficit disorder." His voice faded away like he was a train that had just entered a long tunnel, getting further and further away. Then his words were audible again, "…ADD has different traits in girls than it does boys…and you may have heard of ADHD…(voice fades and then returns again)...but we don't usually see the resemblance of the hyperactivity portion of the disorder in girls…(fades again)." Suddenly, his voice came back loud and clear, and I noticed his eyes looking directly at mine, his white teeth behind his bearded smile. "It's a lot to take in, so let me go through each assessment, and let me know if you have any questions along the way." My ears sharpened, my posture straightened, and he had my full attention again.

He spent several minutes reviewing each test, explaining why it was chosen, what it was for, how Kelly's performance was rated, and what the results meant.

"I still don't understand how to help her," I said.

He explained that accommodations were included in the report. These would provide the necessary information for the teachers and me to support Kelly's learning needs. The thirty-minute conversation created the strangest feeling. I felt like I'd been pushed off a cliff with my feet no longer on solid ground, yet I was being told it was okay because a parachute would eventually open and break the fall. I had no idea where I would land and how to get there, but there was a sense of movement and hope for a positive change ahead.

This was good news, I now have the actionable steps we need to help Kelly learn.

It was the first time I had heard the words dysgraphia, dyscalculia, dyspraxia, and attention deficit disorder. It took me back to when, in the hospital emergency room, the orthopedic surgeon explained the next steps with Kelly's broken arm needing plates and screws and the probability of multiple surgeries to keep up with her growth. It was too much, too fast, almost surreal, and not what I wanted to hear! I wanted to hear there was a simple, quick, painless, and inexpensive solution.

I left the office mentally exhausted but lighter on my feet. Kelly and I got in the car. I looked in the review mirror to see Kelly buckle her seatbelt; she saw my eyes and asked, "Momma, did I do okay?" I started bawling and could not stop the tears streaming down my face, but I managed to say, "Baby girl, you did fantastic!" We both laughed. I put the car in reverse for the last time in this parking lot and started the long drive home.

I now had an accommodation plan and couldn't wait to share it with her school. We finally had a way to help this clever girl learn to read and write!

After Kelly was in bed that night, I sat at the kitchen table and meticulously read Dr. Carlaw's report. I had to stop several times and look up the meanings of the medical jargon for clarification and understanding. Ultimately, the report identified each test that was conducted and its purpose. It provided graphs, charts, and numerical values and listed Kelly's results compared to the "average expected norm." Her results were significantly different in many categories, including reading, writing, and mathematical concepts, and there were listings of various "deficiencies" such as cognitive comprehension processing, executive functions, and memory recall. You can find more specifics of this test on the neuro-navigation.com website.

RESEARCH INFORMATION:

Seeking External Professional Support:
Specific Learning Disabilities are neurodevelopmental conditions that affect a child's ability to understand or learn information.[1] Significant challenges with math, reading, or writing each characterize their own specific learning disability. Specific learning disabilities are different from attention deficit hyperactivity disorder (ADHD), in which children have trouble sitting still or staying on task in school.

Symptoms of specific learning disabilities include a slow reading speed for your child's grade level, trouble understanding the meaning of what they're reading, struggling to write out thoughts without grammatical errors, a marked difficulty with spelling, particular trouble with mathematical concepts like addition, subtraction, multiplication, and division, and difficulty completing math problems or knowing how or when to apply the concepts.[1]

If you are concerned about your child's learning development or behavior, it is recommended that you speak with your child's pediatrician or school psychologist. They can help you determine if further evaluation is necessary and recommend a specialist if needed.

Professionals, including psychologists, psychiatrists, and medical doctors, may conduct assessments to

reach an accurate diagnosis. These licensed professionals utilize a combination of standardized assessments
alongside interviews to conduct a comprehensive evaluation. Diagnosis typically involves thoroughly reviewing
the child's behavior, cognitive development, and medical history.

Neurodiversity Testing:
Receiving a clinical diagnosis helps remove the barriers to getting the tools and resources needed to support
your child's learning goals. However, it does not always
guarantee an auto-pilot response to adhere to the plan
at the local school district. First, it's essential to
have a diagnosis from a credible source.

A diagnosis involves neurodevelopmental screening
and assessing an individual's medical and behavioral history by a credentialed specialist. These tests can help
parents and individuals who suspect they may be neurodivergent by assisting them in identifying core traits and
areas needing more support. Generally, the responsibility of testing children for neurodiversity falls on the
parents or guardians of the child. However, schools or
healthcare providers may also be involved in the process.

Untreated learning disorders can have far-reaching
consequences beyond academic performance. These reper-
cussions encompass heightened risk of psychological
distress, compromised mental well-being, unemployment,
underemployment, and school dropout rates.[2]

It is important to note that there is no single
test for neurodiversity. There are multiple assessments
for the different conditions to diagnose neurodivergent
learning disabilities. Clinical professionals use more
than one test to confirm their diagnosis, and tests are

determined based on what is most accessible for the patient. For example, Dyslexia is a learning disability that affects reading, writing, and spelling skills. There is no single test that can diagnose dyslexia. The diagnosis for dyslexia is based on a combination of factors, including patient history, reading tests, neurological tests, psychological examinations, and aptitude tests.

A list of neurodevelopmental assessments and diagnostics can be found in the appendix.

REFERENCES:

[1] "What Is Specific Learning Disorder?" n.d. https://www.psychiatry.org/patients-families/specific-learning-disorder/what-is-specific-learning-disorder

[2] "LD Basics." n.d. Promise Project. https://www.promiseproject.org/promise2/learning/ldBasics

ACTION ITEMS:

1. Ask your child's pediatrician for a referral to a neuropsychologist specializing in educational diagnostic services. An external expert will be valuable for a non-biased evaluation.

2. Make the cognitive exam appointment and bring back the results to your child's school and medical doctor, asking for their thoughts on the next steps.

3. Request your school psychologist to review the documents and establish an official Individualized Education Program for your child.

DREAM, ADVOCATE, AND WATCH AS YOUR HARD WORK WILL TRANSFORM YOUR VISION INTO A REALITY!

CHAPTER 6

BRIDGING THE GAP: ADVOCATING FOR LEARNING ACCOMMODATIONS

On the third day, when I finished the tests, Dr. Carlaw invited my mom from the lobby to join us in the purple room. He said he had the results of all the tests. My heart sank; I thought I would be in trouble again—I just knew I probably didn't get the correct answer to the questions. Then, I heard Dr. Carlaw say that I had specific learning disabilities. He was super kind when he explained that we are each unique and that sometimes our bodies need support to help them. He said it was like how I had green eyes and he had brown eyes. He continued the comparison by saying that something inside his eyes makes him need to wear glasses to see things that are far away and that sometimes people need different kinds of support to help them read or do schoolwork. He told me my specific learning disabilities caused me to need support so I could do schoolwork. And then he said my support was called "accommodations," he pointed at a stack of papers and said, "And I have them right here."

He then turned to my mom and started talking to her, showing her the papers. While they were talking, I started thinking about how I wanted to read more than anything! I knew everyone in class could read but me, and now I thought maybe I could, too. I just needed different support….something called accommodations—this was good news!

I overheard Dr. Carlaw say my specific learning disabilities made me unique and meant that I thought about things and learned things differently from other kids in my class. It wasn't a bad thing, but it meant that sometimes teachers and parents need information to understand what helps kids like me to learn. Just like he needed glasses, I needed accommodations at school so I could learn, too. One thing I was most relieved about when he talked about my accommodations was that my teachers would not surprise me by asking me to read out loud in class. This was especially hard for me, and he explained that these stressful situations made my brain respond with something called a fight or flight reaction. When this happened, I was not able to concentrate or respond appropriately.

I was so relieved, but I really didn't completely understand why, except that Dr. Carlaw was the first adult who seemed not to blame me and said how others could help me learn.

When I returned to school, Mom walked into the classroom with me. As I went to my desk, I heard my mom tell my teacher about Dr. Carlaw and my new accommodations. I thought, "Wow, things are going to get better from this day forward!" He and my mom told me how the accommodations would help the teachers understand that I learn differently. This is how I turn my reading powers on!

Unfortunately, even after I visited Dr. Carlaw, I still had terrible days at school, and they were actually getting worse!

About two weeks after my visit with Dr. Carlaw, I submitted my Scholastic Book Fair orders to my regular classroom teacher before we did the pledge of allegiance.

She seemed very pleased with my long list of orders and the fat envelope I gave her. For the past weeks, as instructed by the school, I had been going to all my Mom's friends to show the order book. My Mom's friends were always so nice and they picked something out of my catalog to buy.

Later that same week I turned in my Scholastic Book Fair stuff, the teacher announced in our classroom that I and another girl were recognized for the most Scholastic book orders. She explained that the prize for the most orders was the winners got to spend the morning with the assistant principal, and each of our homeroom classes would get to celebrate with a pizza party. The class cheered when she menionted the pizza party. This was all exciting until the day it happened.

On the morning of the Scholastic Book Fair recognition, the winners were sent from their separate homerooms to the assistant principal's office. I wasn't sure how to get there, so another kid walked me. Once at the assistant principal's office, the other winner and I were asked to stand at her desk while she said our names during the morning announcement. These announcements could be heard in every classroom through the PA system. After she said my name, she asked me to speak into the microphone and answer what my favorite book was. I didn't have an answer. She told me to think about it and then asked the other girl. Eagerly, the other winner got up close to the microphone and said, "Geronimo Stilton"! The assistant principal seemed pleased and asked her what she liked about those mouse detective books. The girl answered as she leaned into the microphone again.

Next, the assistant principal described the books on her desk in the microphone and said, "Kelly, you get to pick out any book you want to keep. What book are you going to pick?" I pointed at one of the books with animals on the front cover, and she put the microphone up to my lips and whispered, "Please read the book title so they know what you picked." I looked at the book in my hands. It was yellow, with red letters that were floating and overlapping. I felt my face get very hot. I opened my mouth, but nothing came out. It felt like time slowed down. I looked for the door and saw it was closed. Then, I heard the assistant principal read the title of my book. She then moved the microphone and asked the other girl to pick hers out and read her book's title. She did. The assistant principal then announced someone was going to do the remaining morning announcements. She clicked her microphone off, and you could hear outside of her office, someone talking on the PA system, asking everyone to stand for the pledge of allegiance. Instead of doing the pledge, the other winner and I were told to sit in the chairs across from the assistant principal's desk. She talked to us for a while about what we were going to do for the morning. We mostly stayed in the administrative office and talked to the other people who worked there, learning about what they did and how we could help if we wanted to.

After spending the morning in the administrative office, we took our prize books and returned to our separate homerooms to enjoy the pizza party.

When I returned to my classroom, the class clapped for me, and I held up my new book. Then I heard someone say, "That's a book for babies"! The teacher said, "Let's give another big round of applause for Kelly…" When the pizza arrived, I sat alone at my desk, eating my slice of pizza, and decided I never wanted to look at the animal prize book again.

As I picked off the mushrooms, I thought to myself – It didn't seem like things were getting better at school.

MOM'S PERSPECTIVE:

The next school day, after we received Kelly's test results, I took a copy of Dr. Carlaw's report to Kelly's school.

After glancing at the report, her teacher said, "This is what we need." She explained that she would give the report to the school psychologist, and someone would contact me to set up an "IEP" meeting (I didn't know what that meant). I later learned that it was an acronym for the Individualized Education Program. As I left the school, I waved a sad goodbye to Kelly, thanked the teacher, and waited for the next steps.

And waited. A whole week after providing Dr. Carlaw's cognitive evaluation to the teacher, I still had not heard anything regarding the "IEP" meeting, and Kelly could not tell that anything had changed in her classroom instruction, so I went back to the school to inquire. I asked for the school psychologist this time and learned they were on leave of absence but would be returning early the following month.

So we kept waiting.

Finally, seven weeks after the date of the diagnosis letter, I received a phone call to meet and discuss Kelly's "IEP." I understood that the meeting was to include multiple people, so it was planned for the following month to coordinate everyone's "busy schedules." We agreed on a date. Before I hung up, I asked a question.

"What does 'IEP' mean?" When we met in person, I was assured the school professionals would handle and explain everything regarding the Individualized Education Program.

But when Kelly's IEP meeting finally came, I felt out of my league and overwhelmed by all the people packed into the small school conference room. The principal, vice principal, special education department lead, school counselor, school psychologist, every teacher Kelly currently had, and someone from her presumed future middle school were present.

And me.

I was greeted warmly as we started with a flurry of names and titles, some of which surprised me. For example, the school psychologist was different than the school counselor, but I did not know how or why a school had these roles.

After the introductions, the school psychologist handed out a packet of papers. She guided us through the packet briefly, explaining something and then directing us forward to another page, but it felt like I was in an advanced college-level class. The jargon was new, the acronyms were abundant, and the presence of authority and decision-making felt one-sided. Two attendees kept looking at their watches during the meeting, and one left before the hour-long conference concluded.

The packet was 30 pages long, and we spent a maximum of 15 seconds on most pages. Some of the pages were skipped.

As I flipped through the pages, trying to keep up, I heard, "Oh, that's just boilerplate information; we want to focus on page 28." The conversation began with the school psychologist explaining the assessment he had conducted on Kelly. While he walked us through the information on page 28, I vaguely understood that the school had assessed Kelly's capabilities since I had provided them with Dr. Carlaw's evaluation. I remember thinking, "If they knew what to test, why had they not done this prior??"

Well, at least we are all here today to make Kelly's failed education a priority, I thought. The school psychologist said that his evaluation agreed with most of Dr. Carlaw's accommodations and instructed us to flip to the accommodation page to start reviewing them.

My brain felt overloaded from the multiple introductions and throughout the IEP meeting. The experience resembled being pulled over by a police officer while on your way to work. You hear the words they speak while you are sitting in the car, listening out the window, but your mind is racing, unable to take in the information—and before I knew it, the hour was up.

With everyone smiling again, they required that I sign the last page indicating I agreed with the IEP. The plan was for the school office to share the list of school-approved accommodations—which were drastically limited compared to Dr. Carlaw's list—with Kelly's teachers, get a baseline of Kelly's current academic skillset, and meet again as a team to set educational goals. After I signed the document, it was passed to others around the table who signed it. I was given a copy of the IEP, and we all promptly left the small school conference room.

Still in the school guest parking space, I sat in my car for 20 minutes, re-reading each word in the IEP document. I realized the following meeting timeline was the end of the school year. I went back into the office and asked about the date for the next meeting and was told, "By law, we only have to revisit the IEP once a year." I took her for her words, figuring she knows more than I do, and I returned to my car and thought well, at least we have a direction now for a positive learning environment for Kelly. All will be better now!

As I started my car and began to drive away, I had this nagging thought that waiting a year to meet again seemed wrong and too far away. But they did mention that it was good timing as she would be in middle school with blended programs with more resources for her learning needs by this time. These school experts of titles and advanced degrees thought it best that Kelly continue to spend most of her days in the special education program for the rest of elementary school; they must know what is best. After all, she would now have the accommodations, so her school days would soon be better.

As much as I tried to match my feelings to the confident smiles at the IEP meeting, I remember a strong sense of being unsure. I can only liken the experience to driving my "newly used" car off the used car sales lot and waving back to the salesperson, who briefly became my friend but now was counting the dollar bills in his hand and ignoring my wave goodbye. Hopefully, this is the right decision for Kelly. It is, right?

RESEARCH INFORMATION:

Understanding the IEP:
An Individualized Education Program (IEP) is a critical document for children with disabilities and is required by law to be reviewed at least once every 12 months. Creating the document can take multiple meetings, as

every child and their needs are unique. It is essential to ensure that educational goals are included and services are detailed to meet the child's current needs. Parents or guardians can request an IEP meeting anytime if they feel changes are needed.

Parents of children with learning disabilities must learn to effectively navigate the maze of special education laws and advocate for their children. Information is power. Leveraging the school experts is wise, but it should not be the only means to discovering success for your child's learning needs.

Ask Lots of Questions and Listen to Answers:
Become like a reporter: Ask questions like, "Who, what, where, when, why, and how?" Listen carefully to the answers you receive and ask for information to be provided in writing.

Document your understanding of the responses instead of relying on your memory to ensure agreement and clarity of decisions and next steps.

Do your best not to come across as antagonistic or defensive. Aim to be open and honest in your replies, keeping in mind the goal of creating positive pathways to success.

Here are some examples of questions to ask in your first IEP meeting:

- What are my child's strengths and weaknesses?

- What academic goals has my child achieved so far?

- What types of modifications are recommended for my child?

- What are my child's school goals for this period?

- What progress has my child made toward school goals?

- What adjustments or changes does my child need to be successful?

- What do the supports look like daily?

- What can I do at home to support their goals?

- What's my child's current educational plan?

- Can we exchange contact information?

Know Your Rights:
Two laws that govern special services and accommodations for children with disabilities:

1. The Individuals with Disabilities Education Act (IDEA)

2. Section 504 of the Rehabilitation Act of 1973

Learning about each is essential for effective advocacy.

The Individuals with Disabilities Education Act (IDEA) guarantees each eligible disabled child a free appropriate public education (FAPE) that emphasizes special education and related services designed to meet the child's unique needs. The vehicle for providing FAPE is through an appropriately developed individualized education program (IEP).[1][2] Essentially, this equates to equity access to education.

When an IEP is appropriately developed and effectively implemented, neurodivergent learners can experience social, emotional, and academic success.

IDEA mandates specific obligations for schools to provide a free, appropriate public education (FAPE), including:

1. The entitlement of each eligible child with a disability to FAPE that emphasizes special education and related services designed to meet the child's unique needs.

2. All children enrolled in public schools and children with disabilities publicly placed in private schools by a state education agency are entitled to FAPE.

3. An appropriately developed IEP based on the child's individual needs.

Multi-tiered Support:

The neurodivergent student should receive a multi-tiered system of support from the school to create a comprehensive prevention framework designed to improve developmental, social, emotional, academic, and behavioral outcomes using a continuum of evidence-based strategies and supports.[3] To achieve this, educators may provide one or more of the following:

- universal strategies and supports designed for all children,

- targeted strategies and supports for children with additional needs and

- intensive strategies and supports to meet the specific needs of individual children

Overall, the focus is on meeting the educational needs of all children by using universal screening, progress monitoring, and data-based decision-making at all tiers of a flexible structure that allows schools and early childhood programs to customize and organize practices, supports, and services based on each child's needs.

Roles and Responsibilities:

Recommended roles in reviewing the evaluation and deciding on recommendations to address areas of your child's learning needs should include the neurodivergent student, their parent/guardian, the child's "regular" education teacher(s), the special education teacher(s) of the child, and the school psychologist and counselor.

A representative from each of these areas should attend every IEP meeting, focused on ensuring equity in education access for your child by interpreting and creating implementation strategies based on the evaluation results. The lead of the IEP meeting should be a representative qualified to provide or supervise the provision of specially designed instruction to meet the unique needs of the neurodivergent student, knowledgeable about the general education curriculum, and knowledgeable about the availability of resources.

Areas to Address:

To support the neurodivergent learner and help their teachers recognize and respond to their learning needs, address these specific areas, and advocate their needs at the IEP meeting:

- **Homework**—Are reading, writing, and math skills behind? Are there certain kinds of tasks that they have the most trouble with? What are these and the tools or resources introduced to support your child?

- **Concentration and Focus**—Do you notice unusual time focused on the work? What interventions have been tried to improve focus, and what are the results?

- **Safety**—Are there any safety concerns? Which environments do not feel safe or need more observation for safety?

- **Behavior**—Do you see times when the child behaves differently than expected? Is the behavior new? Does it impact others? Is it concerning? What might be the catalyst for this behavior, and what interventions have been implemented to support the situation?

- **Physical Symptoms**—Share if you have noticed or heard the child's complaints related to sensory irritations or concerns. What has been addressed, and what were the outcomes?

Because masking behavior is typical for neurodivergent students coping with their surroundings, it is essential to ask the student direct questions to discern if they are struggling in school.[4] Here are examples of questions you can ask:

- How do you feel about school? This can help you understand your child's attitude, motivation, and emotions towards school.

- What are you good at in school? What do you enjoy? This can help you identify your child's strengths, interests, and passions.

- What are you finding hard in school? What do you need help with? This can help you pinpoint the specific areas or subjects that your child is struggling with and how you can support them.

- Who are your friends at school? How do you have a good relationship with them? This can help you assess your child's social skills, peer relationships, and potential bullying issues.

- How do you cope with stress or frustration at school? This can help you evaluate your child's mental health, coping strategies, and resilience.

- You can also talk to your child's teacher for more information about their academic performance, behavior, and learning style. If you notice any warning signs that your child is struggling in school, such as declining grades, avoiding homework, losing interest, or having trouble sleeping or eating, you should seek professional help as soon as possible.

Take the time to write the answers, review patterns, and compare your notes. It is valuable to collect this information and use it in an "About Me" child portfolio to share with future teachers as an introduction to your child's needs. An example of an About Me template can be found on neuro-navigation.com or in the Appendix.

REFERENCES:

[1] Individuals with Disabilities Education Act. 2024. "Individuals With Disabilities Education Act (IDEA)." March 15, 2024. https://sites.ed.gov/idea/.

[2] Positive, Proactive Approaches to Supporting Children with Disabilities: A Guide for Stakeholders (July 19, 2022) - Individuals with Disabilities Education Act. https://sites.ed.gov/idea/idea-files/guide-positive-proactive-approaches-to-supporting-children-with-disabilities/

[3] Eesha Pendharkar. 2023. "MTSS: What Is a Multi-Tiered System of Supports?" *Education Week*, October 13, 2023. https://www.edweek.org/

teaching-learning/mtss-what-is-a-multi-tiered-system-of-supports/2023/10

[4] Mia Barnes. 2022. "Masking: What Is It and Why Do Neurodivergent People Do It?" Psychreg. September 13, 2022. https://www.psychreg.org/masking-what-why-neurodivergent-people-do-it/

ACTION ITEMS:

1. Connect with other parents. You will find strength and support in those who walk similar paths and relate to your plight. Looking to connect with others? Join our network at Neuro-Navigation.com.

2. Determine with the experts (students, teachers, and psychologists) what accommodations might work for your child and help your school implement and track the progress.

3. Make sure your child understands their accommodations by practicing them.

4. Know your rights! Your child can access appropriate education for their learning needs.

LEARNING DIFFERENTLY DOES NOT DEFINE YOUR INTELLIGENCE.

CHAPTER 7

TURNING POINT: REACHING THE LIMIT AND FINDING HELP

My first day of middle school was a disaster.

Unlike elementary school, where I had a homeroom and a portable, for the first time, I had a schedule of classes, each with different rooms to navigate.

When I arrived in my first class, homeroom, I was surprised to see so many students in one room. I sat in the first empty seat and watched more kids enter. The bell rang, and the teacher told us to find a seat. Then she announced that we would say "Here" when we heard our name called.

After the roll call, the teacher handed out a paper with the information about our assigned locker. She then told us to go to the hall, find and open our locker, then return to our seats.

This felt like too many instructions all at once for me.

When I asked where my locker was located, the teacher seemed frustrated. She told me to follow the group and look for the number at the top of my sheet next to the word "Locker."

In the hall with the other kids, I asked for help, and a kid pointed me to my locker—153. It would not open. The nice girl beside me explained that I needed to follow the combination instructions on my paper. I tried to follow the picture of directions with arrows going one way and then going the next, but I couldn't figure it out. The same girl saw I was struggling, and she looked at my paper, turned the knob on the lock, and opened my locker.

Ta-Da!—my locker was open! Now what? I watched others go back to the room, so I followed.

I was never able to open that locker again.

When we returned to the homeroom class, the teacher handed out another paper. She explained that it was our individualized printed schedule that listed the class name, classroom number, and teacher name. She said some stuff and asked if we had questions, but it felt like too much information too quickly.

Soon, a loud bell rang, and the homeroom teacher told us to go to the next class and to hurry before the next bell. My next class was science, room A278, Mr. Murray… but I couldn't read it.

As soon as I left homeroom and stepped into the hallway, I felt like I was stepping into a moving herd. I wasn't sure what direction to go, but the crowd pushed me toward the right. I was mesmerized, watching the halls filled with kids and sounds get louder. I was overwhelmed and confused about navigating the sea of people and finding my next class. I pushed my way back into my homeroom class.

The homeroom teacher had just finished talking with another kid. Before I could ask for help, the teacher grabbed the schedule from my hand, pointed at the kid walking out the classroom door, and said, "Follow him to science." I grabbed my paper from her and ran to catch up with the kid wearing the navy blue backpack.

I followed the navy blue backpack through the sea of students. He was tall, had black wavy hair, and his backpack had a brown zipper tag that bounced when he walked, so it was easy to keep an eye on him in the crowd. He walked up the stairs, down the hall, and into a room.

When I caught up to the kid with the navy blue backpack, he was speaking to a teacher inside the doorway. I overheard the teacher say the rooms were changed, and science is now "down the hall in 216." The teacher grabbed the schedule paper from my hand, said, "216... follow him," and pointed at the navy blue backpack kid walking out the door.

I followed the navy blue backpack kid until he suddenly turned and entered the restroom. I was left standing in the hall. The bell rang even louder than last time. I looked around. I was lost.

Then, a teacher came out of a room across the hall and said, "Are you looking for science?" I walked toward him and nodded yes. He waved me to come to his room and unhooked the open door from the wall, allowing it to close slowly. I was the last kid to enter, and the science teacher pointed at a seat, saying, "Take a seat."

At each desk was a big, heavy book. He called each kid's name out and told us to say "Here" when we heard our name. I still wasn't sure I was in the right class, so when he called my name last, I was so thankful and said, "ME — um, I mean here!"

Then he told us to open our book to a page number and read the names of the chapters. He started at the first desk and asked the student to read the title of chapter one of the book.

I could feel my body shaking as I waited for him to call my name. The room got smaller and smaller each time a kid read a chapter title. But right before it was to be my turn, the teacher said, "And the last chapter is all about bugs."

Whew, that was it…he wasn't asking anyone else to read.

He next handed out a piece of paper and asked everyone to complete it. I could tell others knew what they were doing, but I did not. I looked at the person beside me as she was writing extremely fast, and she angrily said, "Don't copy off me!" I heard some kids laugh, and my face got warm with embarrassment.

The bell finally rang, and everyone put their paper on the teacher's desk before they rushed out the door. I just took my blank paper with me and followed out the door.

As I walked out the science classroom door, I realized I had no idea how to get to my next class. I was in a hallway I didn't recognize, and…there was a sea of kids to walk through….the noise of people talking was so intense I could not think. People kept bumping into me. Someone stepped on my heel, and my shoe almost came off. I kept walking, but now I was against the heavy traffic. A doorway leading to a set of stairs appeared to my right, and I quickly ducked in. I sat on the first stair and reached down to put my heel back in my shoe—and the bell rang again.

The halls emptied in seconds, and suddenly, I was alone—no other kids. I was supposed to be in class, but now I was late. I was breathing so hard that every breath echoed in the cavernous silence of the stairwell, and I could hear my heart pounding in my ears. I put my hand on my chest, fearing my heart would pop. I noticed my hands were dripping with sweat. I don't remember exactly what happened, but I was eventually sitting in the nurse's office. I remember the nurse told me to stay put because my mom was on her way to pick me up from school.

In the following days, I continued to feel lost, isolated, and like I didn't belong. Worse, it seemed some of the other kids agreed, regularly calling me names or making fun of me.

I grew tired of the insults—tired of kids saying I was slow or dumb or a "tard." These comments happened every school day, and they slowly ate away at my confidence until there was nothing left.

At one of my lowest points, I thought my life was hopeless and that I would always be too stupid to catch up. Others seemed to think I was too slow and not trying hard enough, so I finally accepted that, no matter what, I was not good enough. I began to feel like nothing or anyone could help me, so why bother trying?

When I think back to the lowest times, I'm reminded of the teacher who asked me weekly to read aloud—each time I panicked. I started to go to every class worried about when the teacher would call on me and ask me to read aloud. My peers laughed at me on the many times I stumbled and stuttered over the words I was trying to pronounce aloud, but the teachers would say, "Keep trying."

Sometimes in middle school the teacher would seperate the class into work groups, and I would be made fun of—or even worse, ignored—by the other students in my group. Each day, in every class, I felt my face warm with heat as I anticipated the worst case of humiliation yet.

Those emotions spilled into lunchtime; I would eat my lunch as fast as possible—I'm not sure I even chewed my food—so I could get outside to the playground. However, there were many times when, instead of joining my class-mates on the playground, I would get ushered away by a teacher to work on some unfinished schoolwork.

I could never concentrate on doing the unfinished schoolwork because all I could hear outside the window was the laughter coming from the playground, and I felt like I had ants in my pants. I couldn't wait until the recess bell sounded so I could stand up and walk around. That's all I wanted to do, but I knew I would get in even more trouble with the teacher if I left my desk before the bell rang.

After the recess bell sounded, I walked slowly to my next class, walking past other kids with smiles plastered on their faces, sweaty hair, and dirty knees coming in from the playground.

The isolation in middle school was more jarring for me but similar to elementary school, where I went to my corner desk feeling lonely.

Back in the classroom, the teacher would say, "Settle down and open up your math book," Separately, the teacher would ask me to put on my bulky white headphones—they were uncomfortable and had a long, annoying plug hang-ing down to the floor. Sometimes, the teacher would put a plastic threefold "blinder" on my desk, saying it would help me concentrate.

I opened my math book and flipped through the pages, looking at the symbols and pretending to be like the oth-ers. When wearing my headphones, I mostly heard my lungs breathing…in and out…in and out… but I could also hear muffled speaking from others in the classroom, as if they were very far away, even though they were only several feet from me. Feeling lonely when you're in a crowded classroom is hard to explain.

It was like I wasn't there—lost on an island—or invisible. I would raise my hand for help, but the teacher would look right through me—she was very busy and often talking to someone else.

I'd keep my arm in the air for a while, switch arms, and then use my other arm to prop it up because it was getting tired and feeling numb.

"Excuse me? Excuse me?" I asked, and my teacher said from across the room, "Put your hand down; I'll come to you in a minute." She said the same thing every day, but she didn't come.

Inevitably—being isolated and ignored, day after day had a physical toll on my mind and body. I started to lose weight and felt nauseated or sick each school day. I threw up before brushing my teeth each morning. I began to feel numb inside and believed things were never going to be different for me. I do not know how to explain it, but I began not to care anymore.

I did not care that I could not do the schoolwork. I did not care that people made fun of me. I did not care about life.

When I told my mom that I was sad all the time and did not care, she took me to the doctor. The doctor did a test called PHQ (Patient Health Questionnaire), and the results made her send me to a mental health therapist and a sleep study doctor. When I went to the mental health provider, she put me on an antidepressant medication after our first meeting, and I had to return every Saturday to talk with her.

At first, the meetings with the mental health counselor were depressing for me. They were an hour long, and she asked me to explain every feeling related to my school or my feelings of not caring about life. Why bother, I thought. Eventually, we talked about my specific learning disabilities, how they made me feel, and how others responded to me. We also talked about how some people, through ignorance, fear, or personal anger, expressed mean behaviors toward people who are neurodivergent or perceived as different, like me.

I learned a little bit about myself in mental health therapy. One of the things I started to understand was that I had something called learned helplessness. Learned helplessness is giving up after facing waves and waves of negative outcomes.

It was the belief that no matter how hard I tried, I could not succeed.

It makes sense why my teachers said I gave up without even trying. It had been proven repeatedly, in most school experiences, that I could not complete the project, comprehend the assignment, or do the homework to the satisfaction of the neurotypical learning standards. Whatever was being asked, taught, and required, I just could not (and never would) be able to do it. No matter how long I stared at the work, how many people "taught" me the lesson, or how many times I guessed at the answer, I was never right. After years of this, I gave up as I did not want to go through exhaustion for the same outcome of failure and disappointment.

As I came to learn from being in therapy several years later, neurodivergent people often face depression, anxiety, stress, low self-esteem, and social isolation. I felt and experienced all of these, sometimes simultaneously. It was also the worst time in my life to have these mental health illnesses because I was so tired of being the problem and needing help. I just wanted to be normal; I just wanted to not hear an adult ask, "Are you okay?" as if I was a huge heavy boulder holding everyone down.

After about six months of mental health therapy and medicine, I recognized my needing mental health therapy was partly due to my harsh environment. I was learning that while I was different, I still had worth like anyone else! I started to see myself a little differently, and I began to have the strength to speak out again. I was now speaking out for myself, not knowing or caring if anyone else could hear, but to hear myself say things like "I'm not feeling happy about this" or "When you speak to me like that, it makes me feel dumb." These were small steps, but they helped me at least tell others that their choices of words were hurtful, so maybe they would not do it to others.

Maybe, just maybe, there was a light at the end of this tunnel.

MOM'S PERSPECTIVE:

On the first day of returning from middle school, Kelly walked through the front door, dropped to the ground, and had a full-blown anxiety attack. She never threw tantrums as a child, so it was highly concerning to watch her scream, purposely hit her legs with a closed fist, and then start hitting her head! All while screaming, "I'm so stupid!"

I felt horrible but didn't know how to help. I gave her space and offered her a cushion from the couch. After she regained control, I asked her if she wanted to discuss it. She never explained why or what had happened. She chose to go to bed early that night.

Later that week…"Mama, what is a tard"? When I heard this question from my daughter, my heart broke. I asked where she heard the word, and she said kids at school started to call her this. Once again, she was calling out for help, sharing that the environment she was enduring was not only a stressful one because of her learning challenges, but the aggression from her peers also compounded it. I shared my concerns with school staff, but as usual, they brushed it away with excuses—too many children and not enough supervision. Or they suggested having Kelly stay close to a teacher so the insults she faced would be easier to address.

It weighed Kelly down and transformed a curious, outgoing, and happy child into someone who lacked confidence and had little interest in going out, having friends, or showing other signs of happiness. When the pediatrician noticed this behavior change, she recommended a clinical psychologist specializing in children with learning disabilities.

After about a month of trying to find a mental health provider with the time and specialty to see Kelly, we went every Saturday. I met with the provider for the first time, and then afterward, she and Kelly met for a full hour.

At first, Kelly approached the meetings with apathy. She didn't care either way or about anything.

After a month of visits, I asked the provider whether these visits were even making a difference—what were we expecting to see as a result? She said it would be up to Kelly to determine the difference. While I did not find the provider's response encouraging, I did appreciate that, slowly, Kelly started talking about each visit on the drive home. I could see a shift in her. She was listening and connecting the dots, helping her understand what she was experiencing.

Kelly was also taking medication for her depression. She tried three different medications for just over a year. But she said she did not notice a difference when taking them and decided to stop. While antidepressant medication can undoubtedly be a source of support for many people, Kelly's mental health did not seem to improve with the antidepressant medications. More than anything, it was time spent with the mental health provider who encouraged Kelly that she was not alone. She was validated in feeling lonely and praised for her endurance and courage to seek deserved happiness with her authentic self. After several sessions, Kelly decided not to return, and I agreed as she demonstrated a newfound strength. At about that same time, we discovered that the public school—finally!— was starting to make progress in the many efforts to embrace and support her accommodations and learning disability needs.

RESEARCH INFORMATION:

Emotional Disability:
An additional barrier to learning:
It is necessary first to note that neurodiversity does not translate to a mental health disorder. Likewise, neurodivergent individuals do not necessarily have poor mental health. However, due to social expectations and a lack of support at school, neurodivergent students may be susceptible to mental health problems—especially in environments where differences are not understood and respected. [1] School can be an anxiety-provoking environment for neurodivergent students. Many face cognitive, sensory,

and social challenges in the school environment, which is usually designed primarily with neurotypical students and staff. Continued negative stressors can lead to an added barrier to learning called emotional disability.

Emotional disability is a term used to describe a condition that adversely affects a child's educational performance.[2] It is defined as "A condition exhibiting one or more of the following characteristics over an extended period and to a marked degree that adversely affects a child's educational performance."[3]

Emotional Disability:

• An inability to learn cannot be explained by intellectual, sensory, or health factors.

• An inability to build or maintain satisfactory interpersonal relationships with peers and teachers.

• Inappropriate types of behavior or feelings under normal circumstances.

• A general pervasive mood of unhappiness or depression.

• A tendency to develop physical symptoms or fears associated with personal or school problems.

Social Isolation and Mental Health:
The social isolation that often accompanies neurodivergence compounds the effects of emotional disability. It is important to note that students with disabilities are frequently isolated from their nondisabled peers, and this can have detrimental outcomes.[4] Isolation is a common issue faced by students with disabilities who are routinely educated in settings away from their nondisabled peers with little regard for damaging outcomes.[5]

According to the American Psychological Association (APA), social isolation can lead to adverse health consequences such as depression, poor sleep quality, impaired executive function, accelerated cognitive decline, poor cardiovascular function, and impaired immunity at every stage of life.[6]

According to a 2020 Policy Analysis for California Education report, students with disabilities are routinely placed in segregated classrooms and schools.[7] This pooling of students without regard to their learning needs creates another isolation layer. Research has shown that all students benefit when children with disabilities are included with their nondisabled peers. Creating teaching methods that meet all learners' needs is ideal for inclusion and comprehension of subject matter. Young students with and without disabilities paired as reading friends have been found to help each other academically and socially. However, if this is not structured and modeled well, then students who learn differently become more vulnerable to being bullied or suffering from social exclusion in school. For many students with disabilities, isolation is the standard practice and leads to multiple barriers to receiving a primary education.

Shame and Neurodivergence:
Shame is a common emotion that everyone experiences at some point. It is feeling unworthy, flawed, or disconnected from others. Shame can be caused by unrealistic expectations, negative body image, and being viewed as unintelligent due to a learning disability. It is essential to understand and share the realization that shame is a normal human emotion and that it is okay to feel it. Encouraging neurodivergent individuals to reach out to

someone they trust and share their stories can break the cycle of shame and start a process of healing. Remembering and reminding others that everyone experiences shame at some point is essential. It is necessary to regularly encourage neurodivergent learners to be kind to themselves and practice self-compassion.

Emotional Regulation:

Emotional regulation is an essential skill for children who are neurodivergent. It can help them manage their emotions and thus improve their mental health. When a child can better regulate their emotions, there is often a reduction in the frequency of meltdowns, outbursts, and other negative behaviors.

Parents and teachers can help children develop emotional regulation skills by becoming role models and creating supportive environments. Here are some strategies that aim to increase a child's ability to manage their emotions[8]:

- **Accurately Label Feelings:** Children should be taught to recognize their feelings as they come. A more complex emotional vocabulary adds nuance to our emotional experiences. If you only know "anger," any similar emotion becomes "anger." If you recognize, in a more subtle way, when you feel "annoyed," "anxious," "sad," "frustrated," or "disappointed," you more accurately pinpoint your experience.

- **Normalize Emotions:** All emotions exist for a reason, so ignoring them is not beneficial. For example, anger keeps us safe in certain situations, and sadness signals to those around us that we need support. Emotional maturity develops over time; it is typical for younger children to struggle with it. Read books, discuss emotions, and describe your feelings to your child.

• **Encourage Coping Strategies**: Children can benefit from calm support from caregivers and learn coping strategies such as deep breathing, which helps them identify and label their emotions.

• **Consult with a Psychologist**: Consulting with an experienced psychologist can help children learn critical skills like executive functioning and emotional intelligence. Most schools include a psychologist in their staffing model. Or, if it is more reliable, search for a psychologist on the internet specializing in these skill sets.

Self-esteem and Outcomes:
Bullying is common in schools, but children with learning disabilities are a frequent target; this can also compound mental health struggles.[9] The Learning Disabilities Association of America reports that individuals of all ages with learning disabilities and ADHD are subject to ridicule from peers and are often the objects of bullying behaviors. Furthermore, low self-esteem is a frequent by-product of learning disabilities. School failure leads to disassociation from school settings, and adolescents and teens with learning disabilities who do not receive proper academic support and services run a higher risk than average of becoming involved with tobacco, alcohol, and drugs. School drop-out is linked strongly to functional illiteracy; teens who drop out are at elevated risk of becoming teen parents or involved in illegal activities that lead to potential incarceration. Teen addictions, aggressive and other anti-social behaviors,

and risky pregnancies are therefore linked to learning disabilities and ADHD.

REFERENCES:

[1] "Neurodiversity: Mentally Healthy Schools." n.d. https://mentallyhealthyschools.org.uk/factors-that-impact-mental-health/vulnerable-children/neurodiversity/#

[2] Karmen Tamika Kizzie. "It's Just a Disability" or Is It?: Stigma, Psychological Needs, and Educational Outcomes in African American Adolescents with Learning-Related Disabilities." http://deepblue.lib.umich.edu/bitstream/2027.42/64784/1/ktkiz_1.pdf.

[3] Hassan Maajeeny. "Children with Emotional and Behavioral Disorders in Saudi Arabia: A Preliminary Prevalence Screening." (2018). https://doi.org/10.46827/ejse.v0i0.1550.

[4] Sarah Lynn Auer. "Teachers Expectations for Students with Externalizing and Internalizing Behaviors." (2014). https://core.ac.uk/download/215261315.pdf.

[5] Special Education Silos Hurt Students With Disabilities — Giving Compass. https://givingcompass.org/article/how-to-drive-progress-on-inclusion-for-students-with-disabilities

[6] Amy Novotney. n.d. "The Risks of Social Isolation." Https://Www.Apa.Org. https://www.apa.org/monitor/2019/05/ce-corner-isolation

[7] Commentaries, EdSource. 2022. "Stop Isolating Students With Disabilities." *EdSource*,

February 11, 2022. https://edsource.org/2022/ stop-isolating-students-with-disabilities/667500

[8] Emotional Regulation in ADHD Children: How to Teach Control. https://www.additudemag.com/ emotional-regulation-skills-adhd-children/?fbcl id=IwAR0FyfkMhXtHXXwSOcSdrj2TV9waCsihzSOWlaxRwQ PpJ7nrOKzpP9EpsAY

[9] "Learning Disabilities — Learning Disabilities Association of America." n.d. https://ldaamerica. org/disability_type/learning-disabilities/

ACTION ITEMS:

1. Practice speaking positive affirmations with your child every day. Each morning and evening, take the time to recognize and say positive words about your child.

2. Play with your child every day. Isolation and loneliness take a downhill emotional toll on children who learn differently. Spending time with them allows them to practice their emotions and discover something they like to do.

3. Try something new together. A new place, food, or game gives new experiences and allows your child to expand and find that the world is big and not limited to school experiences. Use this as an opportunity to recognize strengths, provide resources to develop further, and encourage growth in these strengths.

CLAP FOR YOURSELF BECAUSE OTHERS MAY NOT RECOGNIZE OR UNDERSTAND YOUR INCREDIBLE ACCOMPLISHMENTS!

CHAPTER 8

DISTRACTIONS: DISCOVERY OF STRENGTHS FOR SURVIVAL

Pictures, for me, were a necessary connection to communication. I depended on pictures to "read" books and relied on the images for inclusion during storytime. Therefore, it was natural for me to appreciate photography.

For fun one year, Mom entered a photo-taking contest at our local community center. I took pictures with a cell phone camera, and most of the pictures I entered in the competition were of exciting bugs I had found around our neighborhood. I was surprised to learn I had received first place for my grade! I was awarded and recognized for my close-up of a frog eating a cricket! My picture was blown up and put on the community center wall along with other winners. You could see it as soon as you walked in the door of the community building.

On my next birthday, I got a digital camera. I learned everything I could about it. I began playing with different lens settings and learned to set my camera's aperture, manually focus, and other distinct functions. The following year, I asked for and received different lenses, which allowed me to gain a lot of experience with lighting and framing. I love taking pictures of animals or structures at the beach and in the forest, and I sometimes use my wide lens for landscape pictures. I took my camera outside as much as I could. If it was raining, I just walked around the house and practiced capturing different shapes or patterns in various lights. When I was on vacation and taking pictures, other photographers would be interested in what I was doing, and they were always very encouraging and complimentary of my photos. I felt like I was part of the photographers' club. It was the first time I felt welcomed and like I could be myself.

When I turned sixteen, my mom and I put together a website called VanZant Imagery, where I could upload all my pictures. Over the years, I upgraded my camera a few times and now have more lenses than will fit in my camera bag. Soon, I started to get requests to take photos for engagement announcements, senior photos, and fundraising events that included a Gala for a large nonprofit hospital in our community. I never got paid very much, but I liked the opportunities to help others. I got to practice improving on my distinctive style, and, best of all; I heard that my customers were pleased with my professionalism and the pictures I took for them to capture their beautiful events. Finding this passion and pouring my energy into it was a lifesaver. It was a distraction from the daily struggles in school and the reality that I could not read, write, or do math.

Talking about my photography business, working on my pictures, or doing a photoshoot were happy and satisfying experiences. I felt good talking about photography with people I would otherwise be incredibly intimidated to be in the same room with for fear they would learn I could not read or write. I appreciated the constructive criticism and hearing thoughts on how my pictures could be even better. Many told me I had a natural eye for framing and capturing attractive and desirable photos. I knew what I liked and tried to take the best pictures to show others what I saw. I remember driving down the road with my mom, and I would say, "Mom, do you see that?" She would not, so I started taking pictures of what I saw to help her know what I saw. That is what I like best about photography—it allows others to see the world like I do. That was huge for me, and once they saw it through my lens, they were so delighted that I felt like I had something to offer and that people just needed help understanding me.

Finding this strength in photography and receiving encouragement from others gave me a sense of belonging and value. I could understand, explore, and grow my knowledge and skills for the first time in a long time. I could communicate with others about my photography knowledge, and I found it exciting that people were genuinely interested in what I had to say.

Sometimes, I met someone who made it evident that they knew much more than I did in the field of photography, and when that happened, I just appreciated their insight and aspired to one day have that same experience and knowledge to share. I worked on my website and learned lots of skills in web design, and I learned a little about sales, tracking expectations, and setting up photoshoot events on the calendar. Photography was the only joy I had for a long time, and I was *so* grateful for it!

MOM'S PERSPECTIVE:

Navigating the school environment was chipping away at Kelly daily, year after year. But photography brought her so much happiness and empowered her self-advocacy skills.

She worked to understand and master the techniques needed to create beautiful photographs, and her knowledge enabled her to contribute to the art of photography. With photography, she wasn't considered weird or stupid; she was just Kelly.

I reminded her of her photography accomplishments when she shared the name-calling or other struggles from her school days. She started to see that she was clever and had natural strengths that were both valuable to others and herself.

As her business continued to evolve, her confidence grew, and she also started to speak up at school for her needs. She began participating in her Individualized Education Program and the meetings where we had to review and define the accommodations she needed. She started to understand these better, and when they did not happen, she asked teachers if they could help.

These successes empowered and encouraged her to understand the depth and breadth of her needs. She knew that she wanted to learn what was being taught and that accommodations were the key to her comprehending—obtaining, understanding, and remembering—that essential information.

On occasion, Kelly would have a teacher who was uninterested in understanding or supporting her accommodation needs. She and I would role-play, and she would try again with the teacher when she felt brave. If she continued not to get accommodations met, we would meet with the principal, assistant principal, or special education department administrators to share the situation and ask for recommendations for improving the situation. On one occasion, she was moved to a different teacher. Otherwise, it just took one special meeting to ensure classroom teacher accommodations adherence. Kelly spoke very clearly about her needs and why the accommodation impacted her ability to learn the subject. She always offered open conversational approaches.

I found it essential that her voice was being heard and that she expressed ideas and information directly. She was sometimes shy and said she couldn't perfectly voice her needs. Still, with practice, she learned that she didn't have to be perfect with the terminology if she could express the need and how she experienced it helping, just like when she spoke about her photography, when she was authentic, people wanted to listen and learn from her.

RESEARCH INFORMATION:

It's vital for children with specific learning disabilities to cultivate self-advocacy and self-determination skills. These skills help children become more independent, confident, and self-confident academically and personally. Self-advocacy is the ability to speak up for oneself, while self-determination is the ability to make choices and decisions that affect one's life.

The National Center for Learning Disabilities has highlighted the importance of self-advocacy and self-determination in personalized learning systems.[1] The report emphasizes that new education models cannot succeed without explicit attention to developing students' capacities to self-advocate and act self-determinedly.

Parents can play a crucial role in promoting self-advocacy in their children with SLD. They can help their children learn to talk about their unique needs and find opportunities to practice self-advocacy and leadership skills at school, in their house of faith, with friends, and through community organizations or other programs.

Educators are also responsible for providing a climate conducive to student development and exercise of these skills. Each identity a student brings to this process creates a new layer in this dynamic process. For example, helping an English learner who has a learning and attention issue demonstrate self-advocacy is a different task than assisting a student who identifies with only one of these attributes.

It is important to note that each time a student's disability intersects with another learning obstacle—whether it is cultural or racial minority status, poverty, or another identity—educators should reflect on what the student's specific circumstance demands of the student to become a better self-advocate.

Self-advocacy and self-determination are essential skills for neurodivergent learners to develop. These skills can help them become more independent, confident, and successful academically and personally. Self-advocacy can start anywhere and often begins with identifying a strength or keen interest.

One way to promote self-advocacy is to teach children how to communicate their needs effectively. For instance, parents can encourage their children to speak up when they need help or accommodation in school. They can also teach their children how to ask questions, express their opinions, and negotiate with others.

Another way to promote self-advocacy is to help children set goals and make decisions. Parents can encourage their children to identify their strengths and weaknesses, set realistic goals, and develop a plan to achieve them. They can also teach their children how to evaluate their progress, learn from their mistakes, and adjust their plans accordingly.

Still, another way to increase self-advocacy is to explore interests. Allowing the child to explore and identify what they find exciting and enjoy will encourage them to speak about it and share the excitement with others. This builds on communication experiences and expressing emotions in an encouraging exploration.

There are many resources available online that can help parents and educators promote self-advocacy and self-determination in children with ADHD. For example, ADDitude provides a free resource that outlines five steps to more forceful ADHD self-advocacy.[2] This resource includes strategies for building self-esteem, developing a personal self-advocacy plan, mapping out a situational action plan, and keeping a journal.

Open communication with a child with learning disabilities is vital to their development. Here are some tips that can be helpful:

- **Ask Your Child How They Would Like to Communicate**: It is crucial to understand the child's preferred mode of communication. Some children may prefer sign language, while others may use assistive technology.

- **Use Accessible Language**: Avoid jargon or long words that might be hard to understand. Use simple, straightforward language that is easy to comprehend.

- **Let Your Child Lead the Conversation**: Encourage the child to express themselves and take the lead. This can help build their confidence and self-esteem.

- **Ask Open-ended Questions**: Instead of asking "yes" or "no" questions, ask open-ended questions, encouraging the child to elaborate on their thoughts and feelings.

- **Be Patient**: Children with learning disabilities may take longer to process information and respond. Be patient and give them time to express themselves.

- **Use Visual Aids**: Visual aids such as pictures, diagrams, and videos can help children with learning disabilities understand complex concepts.

- **Encourage Social Interaction**: Encourage the child to interact with others and participate in group activities. This can help them develop social skills and build relationships with their peers.

People with ADHD often struggle with "executive function," which is responsible for sorting through the information in everyday life, like organizing your thoughts in the middle of a conversation.[3] Here are some tips that can help:

- **Talking Too Much**: If you tend to manipulate the conversation, try asking questions after you say a couple of sentences to let the other person have their say, too. Silently repeat what is said to you to keep your focus on listening rather than talking.

- **Forgetfulness**: If you have trouble remembering what you would say or what someone else said during essential conversations, document notes or questions ahead of time so you remember what to say or ask. Take notes or ask the other person if using your phone to record the conversation is okay during the talk. If you lose the conversation thread, say, "I spaced out. Can you say that again"? It is much easier than trying to dig for the lost info later.

- **Interrupting**: If you interrupt people without thinking, try counting how often you interrupt a meeting or conversation. Set a goal not to do it more than a certain number of times. If you catch yourself interrupting, own up to it and ask the other person what they would say.

- **Finding the Right Words**: If you have trouble finding the right words during a conversation, take a few deep breaths and try to organize your thoughts. If the right words do not come to you, return to the person later.

ADDitude suggests that patience and understanding are essential when communicating with someone who has ADHD. Using clear, concise language and avoiding sarcasm or negative comments is also helpful. These actions, supported by positive comments, will help build confidence and encouragement for self-advocacy in neurodivergent learners.

Another helpful technique to encourage learning is mindfulness. Mindfulness involves being present in the moment and accepting your thoughts and feelings without judgment. It allows one to observe thoughts and feelings without getting caught up. This can help neurodivergent learners develop a more positive relationship with their authentic selves.

REFERENCES:

[1] "Understanding Self-Advocacy — Learning Disabilities Association of America." n.d. https://ldaamerica.org/lda_today/understanding-self-advocacy/

[2] Jerome Schultz, PhD. 2022. "Free Resource: 5 Steps to More Forceful ADHD Self-Advocacy." ADDitude. April 4, 2022. https://www.additudemag.com/download/adhd-self-advocacy-skills-for-children/

[3] Russell Barkley, PhD. 2024. "What Is Executive Function? 7 Deficits Tied to ADHD." ADDitude. January 29, 2024. https://www.additudemag.com/7-executive-function-deficits-linked-to-adhd/

ACTION ITEMS:

1. Focus on strengths and pour your love and resources into encouraging activities that nurture these strengths.

2. Find and join organizations that nurture your child's interests and support them in navigating the world with learning disabilities.

3. Practice with your child speaking about and advocating for their specific learning disability, including the diagnosis and accommodations. The voice of acceptance and inclusivity must start with you!

IT'S NOT ALWAYS ABOUT WHAT YOU LEARN, BUT HOW YOU LEARN IT.

CHAPTER 9

BREAKTHROUGHS:
FROM ILLITERATE TO CONFIDENT

When I turned 14, I still couldn't read or write my name on a birthday card.

The typical education system hadn't worked for me. After so many years of struggle and failure and my IEP being ignored, my mom moved me to a specialized school where the teacher/student ratio was one teacher to every nine students. Every teacher was trained and credentialed in non-neurotypical teaching techniques.

Several teachers at the specialized school worked with me to help me understand my kinesthetic and visual learning style and the various techniques and resources I needed to process, comprehend, and recall new information. They fully embraced and implemented all of my accommodations from Dr. Carlaw.

I was excited and nervous to start at this new school. But I was not sad to leave my public school and, frankly, I didn't expect anyone at my old school to notice I had left. I didn't tell anyone I was leaving because I didn't have anyone to tell.

The new school was primarily boys, and many said they were on the autism spectrum. There were two other girls, and I immediately made friends with them. They came to me separately, but both were on my very first day. One talked about the music she liked to listen to; the other said she liked my backpack and then asked me a lot of questions. But she asked questions in a way that didn't feel hurtful. We just connected somehow; plus, the environment at the new school was kinder. It seemed all the kids at the new school were so nice! When we had lunch together later that first week, many kids my age sat with me at the same lunch table. There were so many different and interesting conversations. They talked about all kinds of things like hobbies, being afraid of spiders, favorite foods, the latest movies, and even a long discussion about allergies. Sometimes, the teachers sat at our table when there was room. I never had a teacher at my old school sit at the kid's table and just eat lunch with us. It was pretty cool!

One day at lunch, the kids at my table talked about how weird it was that we all got along and how we all were genuinely nice to each other at this school. Some shared what schools they came from and some of their experiences. Others had not been to any other school except this one. One person noted that it felt a lot less mean at this school, and that included teachers as well as students. This comment really made me think and compare my experiences. It made a lot of sense when a junior said the environment at the special school was probably directly related to all the kids being from similar experiences where they were treated unfairly or like they were dumb because they didn't keep up in the regular school. He then said, "I think we all get along because we know how crappy it feels to be bullied" Another kid followed up with a loud voice, "Yeah, you just don't do that sh*t to other kids"!

Within a few months at the new school, letters became words!

For the first time, I could understand some of what was written in my books, and others could recognize the words I had written on paper! Unlike my previous school, I had exciting books that I wanted to read at the new school. Many of them used a dyslexia-friendly font on colored backgrounds. This font and color stopped the letters from overlapping and floating so I could sound them out and read faster. I learned to use an app called Text-To-Speech to capture and translate my words into text. This saved hours on homework, especially when I struggled to write letters and spell words. I had a writing class that was frustrating because I had to trace letters all over again, but for some reason, it was different this time—I understood why this was important, and I saw it making a difference in my ability to write. I struggle with taking notes while listening. For some reason, my brain can't do those two tasks at the same time. But as my special school teacher would always say, "That's okay; we have a little trick that will help"! So I started to use a new accommodation where I record the lecture. This allows me to listen and stop as needed to take notes. I was surprised that teachers could create accommodations, too! When I was doing a test that wasn't assessing my reading skills, my accommodations would approve that I have technology read the test question to me, and I would write the answer. This helped to remove the barriers of my spending time to comprehend the question through my limited reading skills so I could focus instead on what was being tested. This and other accommodations made me feel like I had a chance when there was a test.

Another thing that was helpful for my wiggles was that after every class, and as much as I needed, I could take a lap on the walking path inside the school campus. I'm unsure how, but this seemed to settle my wiggles and helped me focus when I returned to the classroom.

It was almost always the same classroom that I learned in, as the teachers rotated the students and not the other way around. So, I would have reading, math, and even writing classes all in the same classroom. I didn't have to worry about a schedule or keeping track of the bells. Also, the classes were made up of kids of different ages. Kids were put in the grade level of the subject they were working on versus being assigned to a grade based on their age. When I first went to my reading class and saw there were many younger kids, it felt awkward. But before the end of the class, the teacher explained why it wasn't a competition with other students. He said that no one was considered smart or dumb at this school, and each kid was on their own path to be the best they could be! I felt like I was on the same path as the other kids in my reading class, and sometimes, I even got to help someone else! I started to do great on tests, which made me feel clever. I had three main classes at the new school: reading, writing, and math. The new school made it my priority to stay focused on these fundamental subjects before moving on to new ones. I was being taught in ways that made sense to me, and once I caught on, I soon started to learn—quickly. Eventually, I could take other classes like sign language (which I loved!) to satisfy the second language requirement for graduating.

Although I was not autistic, the school's teaching methods supported my learning style by implementing my accommodations and teaching a curriculum that helped me understand each subject, really understand it. This was life-changing.

After the first year, I could write complete sentences and spell about 60% of the words right. After learning to add and subtract, I started multiplication. Most importantly, I began to like to learn, and sometimes, I wanted more homework because I understood it for the first time and got good grades for what I turned in.

By the end of the school year, at age 15, I was reading at a third-grade level and doing fourth-grade math equations. In just one year, I went from being unable to read my name to reading sentences in the *Highlights* magazines I had collected. I learned I loved to write (even if I was not perfect at spelling) and was encouraged to practice my writing with a fun, unique "creative writing" class at the new special school. The new school's methods, encouragement, and inclusion made the difference. I needed to dig deep and understand how

I still found that the advanced subject levels were challenging, especially since I had just started to get good at doing the beginning level. However, my teachers were encouraging and reminded me that I had a lot of time to make up because I was far behind due to my previous school progress. Slowly, I started to like new challenges and felt that nothing could stop me like before. I came to accept that homework assignments or problem-solving took me twice as long to complete compared to most people, and with the help of my teachers, I realized that was okay. What was more important was that I could get them *done;* that was such a victory. I was now getting As and Bs for the work I submitted. These high grades made an enormous difference in my confidence, and before long, I made it my permanent goal to get straight A's!

At the end of my second year at the special school, my reading comprehension was at a seventh-grade level, and I could do eighth-grade math. I felt like the sky was the limit! Because of this progress, I took my first elective class and picked criminology, which was mainly a hands-on class. For the first time, I felt like I spoke the same language as others and liked learning. This class was in a different room, so it also indirectly helped me to adjust to having a class schedule to follow and keeping track of time.

But despite my progress, I slid into a deep depression in my sophomore year. My insomnia became unmanageable, and at one point, I didn't sleep for 96 hours straight. For the first time, I missed a lot of classes that I didn't want to miss, and my loss of appetite caused me to drop below 100 pounds. It was hard to explain to others, but I felt this constant dark and dreary deep core sadness. My mom tried to cheer me up, but nothing seemed to help this time.

I started to see multiple specialist doctors and did another sleep study. I also returned to the mental health counselor I had seen once before. After taking various different medications, my pediatrician decided to take me off all medications in order to "restart" my system. After this and a few visits with my mental health therapist, I finally began to sleep for short periods at night. My mental health therapist thought that the onset of my depression may have been a response to my recent learning breakthrough in my new school environment. At first, this didn't make any sense to me; after all, I was gaining confidence, feeling clever and capable for the first time since- well, *ever!* She explained that because I was finally in a good place, my body and mind started to relax, no longer experiencing the daily stress and trauma. This caused my mind and body to begin to heal. But part of the healing process was dealing with the depth and breadth of the traumatic experiences and constant survival mode I had endured for years and years—my body and mind were trying to catch up with the positive change. She explained that the lack of sleep and waves of extreme sadness was a response to the release of past tension that manifested into psychological and physical symptoms.

I eventually recovered, regained my appetite, made up the missed schoolwork, and finished the school year strong.

At the end of my junior year, my learning was progressing swiftly. This and the recovery process from my last depression episode made me realize I was ready to move on. I learned so much at the special school, including a lot about myself. I had found my voice, knew what I needed to learn, and understood the rights that were protected by the law. My school and my teachers supported my decision to return to the public school environment. The special school staff met with the public school staff on multiple occasions, always including me, for the purpose of setting up the same support that I needed to maximize my learning potential and access equity in education.

I was all set to return to public high school. This was agreeable to me—I wanted to graduate from a regular high school—a school that had sports, dances, and other social activities that the specialized school didn't. I knew how to advocate for my accommodations so I would blend in and be part of the regular classroom now.

MOM'S PERSPECTIVE:

It had been five years since Kelly's neurodivergent diagnosis. Each year, I met with the IEP team to ensure that their education program would meet the needs of Kelly's learning differences. But I felt like I was at a brick wall due to the lack of progress. I lost my patience after receiving yet another letter requesting Kelly attend summer school due to failing classes.

I called the school and asked if I should send Kelly to summer school again and if they would have teachers who would accept and implement her accommodations. The answer was no; they only hired temporary and part-time teachers for summer school. I had had enough! My voice slowed and got louder as I articulated my question about what other options were available to Kelly. The woman on the end of the phone said, "Don't send her." I thanked her with sarcasm and hung up. I sat in the kitchen and repeated those words…don't send her…don't send her. It had never really occurred to me that it was an option not to send her back to the same place.

I was afraid that my child would remain illiterate. She deserved better. She wanted to learn. I couldn't give up either. I was desperate. And I wanted to try something different, something extreme…I was on a new mission—I would remove her from school and find an innovative solution.

I researched and discovered an accredited school one hour's drive south of us that focused on educating autistic children. I made an appointment and met with them. They were tiny, but their success rate was high. Sharing Kelly's situation with the new school, they gladly accepted her and described the approach and expectations for results. I had nothing to lose. I enrolled her in a summer school program to help her get introduced to the new environment. She liked it and shared that the best thing was that the teachers came to her when she raised her hand.

I took on more debt and enrolled her in this specialized private school. I had emptied my savings account to pay for the summer and first two years' tuition. After that, I signed up for payment plans and cut costs everywhere I could. I took on a different job closer to the new school to reduce the travel costs. Times were REALLY tight with this added private school expense. But for the first time, this school was making a difference. Kelly was finally learning to recognize words, and I would do everything I could to support this progress.

And Kelly made *extraordinary* progress.

During the first school year (eighth grade), as we drove the hour-long ride home after school, she excitedly pointed out words on signs and trucks that she recognized. We made it a game to see how many words she could find before we got home.

I could also see her confidence come back, including the whimsical personality she'd once had long before she started public school. When we got home, she wanted to work on homework, show me what she was doing, and ask me to "grade" it and show her any mistakes so she could fix them immediately.

Kelly was on a fast-track learning schedule and expressed how she was feeling proud of herself and what she could do versus the many years of reminders of what she could not achieve due to her learning disabilities. It was increasingly clear that she wanted to learn but did not know how due to her condition. She quickly caught on to concepts when she and her teachers followed the accommodations and listened more than they dictated directions. She gladly worked on homework because she knew it was possible, and she proved she was right! Now that she knew what she needed to learn, she demanded it!

When she met new teachers, she openly shared that she had disabilities, was a diligent worker, and that she wanted to succeed; she insisted on specific resources from a list of accommodations. I watched a young, shy, low-confidence girl turn into a strong, brave woman who rightfully demanded her learning accommodation needs with precise articulation and self-advocacy. She had a dream and was chasing it with all her might!

After much struggle, Kelly had finally uncovered her approach to learning, and I was so proud of her.

RESEARCH INFORMATION:

Emotional safety is a fundamental human need and a crucial building block for healthy interaction. It's the visceral feeling of being accepted and embraced for who you are without fear of judgment or harm. This is especially important for the neurodivergent learner who struggles with a sense of belonging in their neurotypical environments.[1] You can express your feelings and needs without hesitation when you feel emotionally safe. This allows the neurodivergent learner to feel secure in asking questions, authentically expressing a lack of understanding, and keeping a healthy curiosity and a genuine interest to learn. However, when emotional safety is lacking, the neurodivergent learner creates a mask or avoidance around others, and over time, this can build intense psychological distress.

Imagine someone transitioning from an unsafe school environment; feeling threatened or vulnerable was their norm every day, every week, every year. Then, one day, something changed, and they finally felt safe, protected, and capable. Initially, they might experience relief and a sense of security. But what happened earlier sticks with them for a while, and eventually, they break down emotionally due to various factors[2]:

- **Trauma Resurfacing**: Sometimes, being in a safe environment triggers memories or emotions related to past trauma. The newfound safety allows suppressed feelings to emerge.

- **Fear of Vulnerability**: Feeling safe can paradoxically make someone more vulnerable. When they drop their guard, they may confront emotions they've been avoiding.

- **High Expectations**: In a safe space, expectations for emotional well-being are higher. If someone still struggles despite safety, they may feel inadequate or like they don't belong.

- **Unresolved Issues**: Safety doesn't automatically resolve underlying issues. Emotional breakdowns can occur when those issues resurface.

Emotional safety isn't about avoiding discomfort but feeling secure enough to be authentic. Even in safe environments, people can still experience emotional challenges as a result of the interplay between historical trauma and their new, safe surroundings.

REFERENCES:

[1] Carissa Domrase. 2023. "Creating an Inclusive Classroom for Neurodivergent Learners." Edutopia. March 23, 2023. https://www.edutopia.org/article/supporting-neurodivergent-students-school.

[2] Lisa Nosal. 2024. "Why Are Memories of My Past Trauma Coming Back Now?— GoodTherapy.org Therapy Blog." GoodTherapy.Org Therapy Blog. January 9, 2024. https://www.goodtherapy.org/blog/why-are-memories-of-my-past-trauma-coming-back-now-0518155

ACTION ITEMS:

1. Organize the school binders for each class, making sure each contains an accommodation list that the student can understand and share with the teacher.

2. Before starting the new class, email the student's teacher with a list of school-approved accommodations (needs) and cc the special education department lead.

3. Create a pocket binder for each subject that supports the neurodivergent learner's accommodations/needs (e.g., basic calculator, times table, fidget item, etc.) and make sure they are comfortable using it.

YOUR VOICE MATTERS—
LET IT BE HEARD!

CHAPTER 10

SECOND CHANCE:
BACK TO PUBLIC SCHOOL

After some meetings, my school and my mom helped me switch from the specialized school for autistic children to my neighborhood high school. I was looking forward to (and nervous about) seeing kids I remembered from elementary and middle school. I was excited to share with them that I just learned differently and could now read and do the homework from class.

I was still categorized as a special education student in public high school. This also meant that I was routinely separated from the regular class, something that didn't happen at the autistic school. While two of my classes were in the public high school building, much of my education happened in a separate building—the special education building that was at the opposite end of the high school campus, located behind the well-lit and manicured football field. Like my middle school experience, I had some great and not-so-great teachers when back in the public high school. But this time, at least, I felt like I could understand and do the work.

Regular public school was different for me this time because I was better at advocating for my accommodations, articulating my specific learning disabilities, and also recognizing my talents. I knew who to go to when things were not going well in the classroom with the teacher and who to contact when that route didn't support my recognized accommodation needs. I just took each experience one step at a time and used it as an opportunity to strengthen my communication and advocacy skills. I always tried to assume people were coming from a noble intent and either didn't know how to help or felt they didn't have the time. Neither was acceptable for my success in equity to access education.

I continue to believe that the worst feeling is when teachers do not believe in you. Or at least it feels that way when you are overlooked in class. In most of my classes, I was skipped over when the teacher asked questions and told us to raise our hands if we knew the answer. In elementary and middle school, I was so relieved to be skipped or not called on by the teacher for an answer.

But at the specialized private school, I had learned about myself and how it was okay that I learned differently. At that school, every student in the class was called on every day. We helped each other find answers and understand the content before moving forward — truly, no kid was left behind in understanding the subject matter. So, when I was back at my public high school, I felt like I could figure out the problem and contribute with the right answer if only I had my accommodations implemented. After all, this had been proven to work for me while in the special autistic school, and I was not about to lose all the effort I and my teachers had worked so hard to achieve.

Looking back at my elementary and middle school experiences, I think being skipped by the teacher saved a lot of time in the classroom. The teachers would say, "There is a lot to cover today, so put on your thinking caps." This meant to me that if you don't keep up, that is your problem because we are going to keep going full steam ahead in each lesson. The teacher would let some-one else blurt out their answer, and then we would move to the next question. This was different in how the special school advanced lessons. In the special school, we always reviewed how to get to the answer and did not move on until everyone got it. It created a caring environ-ment where we wanted to help each other and see every-one succeed.

One day, shortly after my return to my public high school, we were all told to go to the auditorium. There were whole days of lessons and training for the entire class to focus on the ACT and SAT college entrance exams. I only attended this once, and then the next time, my teacher and another lady said I could go to the library while these classes were happening. They said the ACT and SAT were tests my peers would take but not something I had to do. I didn't understand much later that these tests helped kids to get accepted into university. These class study times didn't happen a lot, but when they did, they were a full or half day. On those days, I was told to keep busy while my peers trained and studied for them. On one occasion, the public school just sent me home early. Here we go again, I thought as I felt like I was in the way and didn't belong.

The following spring, the COVID-19 pandemic started, and my classes switched from in-person to remote. I thrived in this environment; with a simple click of an address link, I felt included in the public classroom in ways I never had before. I also had the bonus of not wor-rying about being misunderstood in hallway conversations between peers. I didn't have to take the stinky and noisy bus to and from school. Plus, for the first time, the public school teachers looked directly at me in an online class. They were talking to *me*…teaching *me*! Having online courses was a total game-changer for me! I recorded every lecture (part of my accommodations) with no background noises or other distractions and listened to the lesson again at night when doing my homework. This new way of learning was great!

I also just enjoyed learning remotely, as it took away many of the challenges the neurotypical classroom causes for my attention deficit disorder. I had my quiet room set up at home. The technology I used for class allowed me to concentrate and listen, and for the first time at public school, I was one of the few who raised my hand or tried to answer the questions, so the teacher selected me a lot to keep a discussion going. I felt included and part of the class, and it felt great to get answers right. In my home setup, I used software to take notes without being made fun of; I had brown noise playing in the background to help me concentrate, I had the ability to stand or sit, whichever I needed and as a bonus, and I had my cat Louis sleeping next to me, so I did not feel lonely. I excelled in all of my classes when the public school went to online learning.

In addition to completing the credits in reading, writing, and math to receive my diploma, I found out in my last semester of public high school that I also needed to take a state history class, earn PE credits, and complete a speech and geometry class. So, Mom worked with the public school to arrange the history, speech, PE, and health classes to be taught in a way I learned. I took the history and geometry class with a private tutor specializing in students with learning disabilities. I took my speech and health classes from schools located in other states (Washington and Utah) because their instructors were trained with skills for teaching/supporting neurodivergent learners. This separation of school for my ability to access equity in education caused me to start class at 7:30 a.m. because of the different time zones, and sometimes I would not finish a class until 9 p.m. However, it was worth it to me because the lessons landed, allowing me to understand the content and pass the exams. At first, it wasn't easy to convince the public school to allow me to take the classes elsewhere. They were quick to approve the curriculum taught, and online learning had been preapproved. However, the principal stated the public school could not pay for the classes. Mom and I agreed that we had come too far not to find a way to make it work. My high school diploma was within reach!

Altogether, it took systems from three states, but graduation was going to happen!

MOM'S PERSPECTIVE:

During one IEP meeting, I reminded the group to consider Kelly's goals in preparing for college. A teacher asked, "Are we sure Kelly wants to attend college"? I shared that she had mentioned it on multiple occasions. Kelly would often say when she could read, she would go to college…." The vice principal of the public school sternly interrupted me and said that my language of "constantly mentioning college in the IEP meetings" was "borderline abusive." As I looked around the room at the many eyes looking back at me, the vice principal continued by saying they had agreed in discussions outside of the IEP meeting that my delusional misdirecting of expectations for Kelly's achievement to attend a four-year college was borderline abusive as I was encouraging something that "Very likely was not possible."

This was a moment in time I will not forget. It dawned on me that these teachers did not believe in her and had established limits for her without her permission.

I lost my calmness and assertively said, "Who the hell are you not to encourage her on her academic dreams? She wants to go to college and believes she might get there. Who are any of you to say it is not possible? Our job is to move the barriers for her and support her as much as possible to allow her to achieve her dreams!"

The room felt cold, and people who had looked at me before were now looking down at the papers in front of them. The vice principal suggested I remain calm and that I misunderstood her comment.

As I gathered my documents from the table, I said, "If Kelly wants to go to college, I will do everything I can to help her make it there. You should be leading the way, not getting in it!"

RESEARCH INFORMATION:

The traditional education system has historically been geared toward neurotypical students or students who most commonly learn in a similar method.

The classroom design, curriculum, and social structure have developed based on the assumption that students develop and learn in a standard format. This has remained throughout the years, even though many within the student body may fall somewhere on the neurodivergent spectrum.

As suggested by the Association for Supervision and Curriculum Development, neurotypical schools need to improve their support for and provide neurodivergent learners with what they need for their education.[1] They explain that public schools are generally not equipped to provide such intensive and systematic approaches to the literacy needs of neurodivergent learners. According to an Education Week analysis, one in five general education teachers feel "very well prepared" to teach students with mild-to-moderate learning disabilities like dyslexia. [2] Special education classes are not necessarily a good fit because they tend to cater to students whose learning profiles and academic needs vary widely.

To help neurodivergent students succeed in a neuro- typical classroom, teachers can incorporate the follow- ing strategies:

- **Connect with Students**: Teachers can spend the first five minutes of class walking around and talking to students about anything unrelated to school. This helps students feel at ease and more comfortable in class.

- **Request and Digest "About Me" Cards**: Students and their families should complete a basic profile on the student's learning needs, interests, and concerns. An example is provided at www.neuro- navigation.com.

- **Relaxation**: Starting class with calming meditation can help neurodivergent students calm their minds and feel less anxious.

- **Movement**: Allowing students to move their bodies in class whenever possible can help them stay focused and engaged.

- **Variety and Choice**: Offering students variety and a selection of course materials can help them stay engaged and motivated.

• **Explicit Feedback:** Providing explicit feedback early and often can help neurodivergent students understand what they need to do to succeed.

In addition, teachers who get to know their students' learning styles and adjust the curriculum to support them experience better outcomes for the individual, the class, and the teaching experience. Encouraging teamwork, allowing accommodation where needed, and creating a classroom environment to break down differences can also help create a well-rounded and inclusive classroom.

Schools that want neurodivergent learners to have equity access to learning opportunities commit to small student-to-staff ratios and daily intensive literacy instruction using evidence-based approaches.

Public schools are legally required to provide accommodations for students with dyslexia under the Individuals with Disabilities Education Act (IDEA) and Section 504 of the Rehabilitation Act of 1973.[3]

The IDEA requires public schools to provide free and appropriate public education (FAPE) to students with disabilities, including dyslexia. This includes providing individualized education programs (IEPs) tailored to meet each student's needs. Parents and teachers alike must agree on what is deemed appropriate so that each student has equity in primary education and achieves the success they need to navigate within their community. This is not a one-size-fits-all solution, and it is up to educators to explore all methods and resources to discern and apply the methodology for neurodivergent learners to succeed.

The federal Individuals with Disability Education Act allows parents to pursue legal action if they feel their local school system cannot meet their children's academic needs. Section 504 of the Rehabilitation Act of 1973 prohibits discrimination against individuals with disabilities in any program or activity that receives federal financial assistance.

REFERENCES:

[1] "Resources." 2024. ASCD. February 2, 2024. https://www.ascd.org/resources.

[2] Corey Mitchell. 2021. "Most Classroom Teachers Feel Unprepared to Support Students With Disabilities." Education Week, September 24, 2021. https://www. edweek.org/teaching-learning/most-classroom-teachers-feel-unprepared-to-support-students-with-disabilities/2019/05.

[3] Andrew M. I. Lee, JD. 2024. "Section 504 of the Rehabilitation Act of 1973: What You Need to Know." Understood. March 12, 2024. https://www. understood.org/en/articles/section-504-of-the-rehabilitation-act-of-1973-what-you-need-to-know.

ACTION ITEMS:

1. You do not have to be an expert overnight or feel alone in an IEP meeting. Find an IEP advocate and get a second opinion on your child's IEP document.

2. Bring an experienced IEP advocate to your meetings, someone who supports your point of view.

3. Check out neuro-navigation.com if you need an IEP review or advocacy support.

**WORKING HARD TODAY
MAKES THE DREAMS OF
TOMORROW EASIER TO CATCH.**

CHAPTER 11

COLLEGE BOUND:
INFINITE POSSIBILITIES

In my final semester of public high school, as seniors, we received weekly emails about college activities. Sometimes, the email would announce that a different college representative would be on campus and available to talk to students. Sometimes, the announcements congratulated a senior's acceptance into a college. Most of the time, the announcements felt like ads that included virtual tours to learn about a college.

Because I was learning remotely, I wasn't sure how to visit a college representative when they were at the school physically. So, I asked my special education teacher about the college representative emails, and he said I did not need to worry about those emails. He was instead heavily focused on getting me signed up with a state assistance program for job support. I asked my guidance counselor about going to college, and he said that most schools require academic excellence and impressive ACT and SAT scores. I remember these exams that my peers had studied for last year, and now I understand why.

I reached out to the state assistant program per my direction from my public school. My mom helped me fill out all of their paperwork, and we had an interview with a case worker. I was approved — but for what? The state assistant representative said that as long as I submitted a report every three months, I would be able to use their services for free. This included help writing a resume, finding appropriate jobs for me, helping with the interview, and helping with the onboarding of the job. Eventually, I stopped filling out the reports (proof that I still had a disability) for this state assistant program, and I was dropped off their list. I never fully understood how they were going to help me achieve my goals, such as going to college.

One glorious day, an art school appeared in my school email inbox. It was another advertisement that was sent to all the seniors, but it felt like it was meant just for me. I selected the link in the email and watched their recruitment video. I had never done art classes outside of a private photography lesson, but I was drawn to the possibility of art school. I showed the video to my mom, and she encouraged me to check it out. That week, afterward, I could not stop thinking about the school; I watched the video again and clicked another link that signed me up to attend an online tour. I told my mom about it, and she joined me on the virtual tour. I was so excited about this college, and after listening to the tour, I knew this was the place for me!

I shared the excitement of the art college with my high school counselor at our next scheduled meeting, but he ignored the subject and asked if I had met with the state program assistance person yet. After I explained that I was approved for the state assistance program, he seemed to listen to the art school I was excited about. He said he had heard of the school, that it was a good school, and he was pretty sure it was a hard school to get accepted in as a student. He was discouraging and

THE CHILD WHO LEARNED DIFFERENTLY

dismissed the idea of me further exploring or talking to him about the art college. He seemed set that the best direction for me was being supported by the state program. I knew he had a lot of kids to help, so I somewhat understood that he didn't fully appreciate what I was capable of achieving.

I asked my mom to help me with the art college admission paperwork. In addition to the paperwork, one of the requirements for applying to this college was to submit something called a "portfolio" of my artwork. I needed to include at least 20 examples of art and then write details for each piece submitted. The details needed to include an explanation of how, why, and when about each piece of my original art. The only artwork I had was my photography. I sifted through the thousands of photographs I had taken to date. It was difficult, but I selected 20 of my favorite photographs, each representing a completely different style of portrait, macro, landscape, nature, abstract, and more! I used my speech-to-text tool to describe each and explain why they were important to me. I saved it all to one big file and named it "Kelly VanZant portfolio." I uploaded the file as part of the admission section on the college website and pushed the submit button. I didn't expect to hear anything back until after I graduated high school.

Seven days later, I received an email from the art college that said I would get a letter in the mail and requested a time be set up to discuss the contents of the letter. I showed my mom when she got home from work. We checked the mailbox every day looking for this letter, and then, sure enough, on the third day, I had a letter from the art college. The letter was addressed to me, was signed by the president of the art college, and stated that the admission committee deemed my artwork as "crafted with precision, skill, and great attention to detail." The letter stated that, based on my portfolio, not only was I accepted to the art college, but they were writing to offer me a "Presidential Scholarship"!

With my mom's help, we immediately set up a time to meet with the art school to discuss the next steps.

When we met with the art school, the admission counselors gushed over a particular photo I included in my portfolio. From the very start of the college admission meeting, I felt like there was only an interest in talking about what I could do versus the usual main focus being on my challenges. One of the college representatives in the meeting and part of the decision acceptance committee seemed as excited as we were that I was accepted to this nationally recognized art school. Mom and I were beaming with smiles before the end of the conversation. We concluded the meeting with Mom, saying, "We need a few days to go over all of this information and paperwork."

Spoiler alert: I was overjoyed to accept the scholarship and attend the art college!

At the next meeting with my public high school counselor, I shared that I had been accepted to the art school and received a scholarship. Without looking up, he said, "Oh, that's nice," and we never talked about it again. I figured he was just busy supporting other kids, and, as he regularly shared, he was "Overwhelmed."

MOM'S PERSPECTIVE:

It felt like the marathon had finally come to an end, yet there was no finish-line tape.

Kelly's graduation from high school was like climbing Mount Everest but looking back; it didn't have to be that way. It's clear to me that if she had been diagnosed earlier, provided with accommodations consistently, and encouraged to build upon her skills, her education in the public system would have been a drastically different experience.

Nonetheless, she endured and even created her own finish-line tape—she was going to college!

Kelly had talked about college for as long as I can remember. She was never clear on what she wanted to go to college for or what she wanted to pursue after college. But hearing from so many adults that she couldn't/shouldn't/wouldn't go to college because she learned differently added to her determination to prove to herself and her naysayers that she was clever and could do it.

While I wanted her to achieve her dreams, I didn't want to see her fall and potentially get crushed. When she was accepted to the college she had researched and was rightly so proud to have been accepted, I honestly thought to myself that it would be really nice just to take a break! Maybe she could try a summer job or even consider a gap year. However, when I saw that determination in her eyes, I knew it was full speed ahead!

I had no idea how she was going to succeed in college. College is a different crowd, with a less structured schedule and independence than she had ever experienced at school before. This was her dream, and if she was determined to do the work, well, the least I could do was cheer her on and support her.

She struggled in her first year of college: so many new students, navigating a large campus, taking subjects that she was not previously exposed to, and participating in classes where it was assumed each student had note-taking and study skills. She worked every night, every weekend, and slowly got the rhythm of identifying what was due and when. She communicated her learning disabilities to every instructor and also stated she would be the hardest-working student they ever saw! And many have confirmed since that she was!

Her passion was proving to herself that she could succeed in college. This goal was everything to her, and I was honored and proud to support her in accomplishing this goal each step of the way!

RESEARCH INFORMATION:

Continued education is an option for the neurodivergent learner; success comes with preparation and selecting the school and program that best meets their needs. Here are some fundamental strengths to figure out how to build upon before starting college:

- **Self-advocacy**: Learn about your rights and accommodations as a neurodivergent student and communicate your needs to your professors and advisors. Your IEP or accommodation will not automatically transfer. However, find the disability department at the college, show/tell them what has helped you achieve academically in the past, and ask what support they can provide.

- **Executive Function Skills**: Skills like focusing, organization, planning, time management, and self-regulation are difficult for most but are especially so for people with learning disabilities and ADHD. So, recognize this, break down the day into chunks, and use resources, tools, and devices to help you practice staying focused, getting organized, managing your calendar, and taking time for self-care.

- **Study Strategies:** Find out what works best for you regarding learning styles, study environments, note-taking methods, memory aids, and test preparation. Set these systems up, and do not let others unintentionally disrupt what is working for you.

- **Support Network:** Seek out peers, mentors, counselors, tutors, and other resources that can provide you with emotional, academic, and social support. The psychosocial impact of being a neurodivergent learner is stressful and can be damaging to self-worth. Finding an experienced mental health counselor who helps work through the added stresses placed on neurodivergent learners as they navigate the neurotypical school system could be life-changing.

Finding the right school is crucial. It is more common for a neurodivergent learner to feel comfortable on college campuses that create inclusivity for those who learn differently. Some colleges specifically cater to people with learning disabilities and ADHD. Liberal arts colleges and community colleges may have accommodations built into their programs and infrastructure. Even with this consideration, selecting the right college is a personal choice that is more easily made when considering preferred learning styles and previous learning environments. For example, some are more comfortable with a small campus versus a large one. Have a friend or family member help you set up a tour of different campus options to understand what might work best for you. Many schools have virtual tours on their websites that share information about their campus and school experience. However, unless you plan to study remotely, it is highly recommended you visit the school before you accept the offer letter or enroll as a student.

After narrowing down a list of desirable colleges, it is time to tackle those applications.[1] If your neurodivergent brain dreads the arduous, multi-step process, you will discover a plan for tracking tasks and reducing stress at neuro-navigation.com.

Selecting your future education and deciding the school you want to attend is a personal decision that takes some time to identify and follow through. Do not feel rushed because of pressure, and do not feel like you cannot succeed because of your disability. You will accomplish all that you set your mind to making happen.

REFERENCES:

[1] IBCCES Learning Community. n.d. "IBCCES Learning Community." https://ibcces.org/learning/college-application-guide-for-neurodivergent-students/

ACTION ITEMS:

1. Improve time management skills to reduce unnecessary stress and prepare for life. I share some tips and tricks specifically for neurodivergent learners in the back of the book and on our website (**www.Neuo-Navigation.com**)

2. Support your neurodivergent learner in acquiring basic financial skills. Understanding more about

money will empower independence and reduce the risk of being taken advantage of. Find a class that is right for their needs.

3. Find the mental and physical support that reduces the buildup of stress for your neurodivergent learner. Help your neurodivergent learner identify and create a routine for these self-soothing opportunities to find relief and regulate emotions.

YOU ARE WORTHY OF YOUR
ACHIEVEMENTS AND READY TO
SEIZE GREAT OPPORTUNITIES.

CHAPTER 12

SILENCING SELF-DESTRUCTION: THE IMPOSTER SYNDROME

When public high school graduation finally came, because of the pandemic, we had a choice between attending in person or participating remotely. If we were going to join in person, there was a limit to how many people could attend.

So, we chose to join in remotely.

Graduation was a live broadcast by Zoom, and my mom went all out in decorating the house and the yard! We had about 15 family members and friends over for the live graduation event. I didn't need to, but I wore a cap and gown, and when the ceremony started, you could hear a pin drop in the crowded living room. We followed along online as soon as the graduation ceremony started. After the introductions of faculty, speeches, recorded presentations, and awards, the principal and other school staff gathered around a table with stacked diplomas. They began to call out names and announced that those participating remotely (me!) would be announced in alphabetical order combined with the students in person. When they called the name of the student who participated in person, that student walked onto the stage, shook the hand of the presenter, and took their diploma. When they called the name of a student participating online, the presenter on the stage waved at the camera, a brief senior picture was flashed on the screen of that graduate, and with a caption of "congratulations" and their name. I was ready for this and had already submitted my picture to display when my name was called. Four hundred-eight students were graduating, so the announcements took a long time.

Finally, the announcement of the students whose last name starts with the letter "V" began. Everyone in my tiny living room got noticeably quiet when it came time to call my name; however, they never called it.

The announcer skipped over my name and went to the next letter in the alphabet.

"WHAT THE HELL?" my mom said.

Once again, I was left out. Part of me was not surprised because, as a disabled kid in public school, this type of oversight of presence was normal. I was more embarrassed as I saw my dressed-up family in the decorated living room staring at me with sadness on their face. My face must have been flushed red with embarrassment when I heard my grandma say, "That's okay, kiddo; we know you did it, and that's all that matters."

She was right; it didn't matter anymore. I felt relief that this chapter was over.

A few days later, my mom went to the school and picked up my diploma. When she asked why my name was not mentioned during the graduation ceremony. The school secretary confirmed we had submitted all the required information and shared that she had a few others make a similar complaint, and they were looking into the mistake. We never did get a reason…or an apology.

After picking up the diploma, we went to our favorite restaurant. When we took our seats across from each other in a familiar booth, we simultaneously let out a loud, audible sigh...and chuckled. The waitress stood at the end of our table and asked the standard question: if we were eating at the restaurant today as part of celebrating a birthday or a special occasion. In unison and for the first time, we answered..."YES"! I waved my diploma in the air and explained that I had just graduated from high school. The waitress smiled and warmly replied, "Wow, that's great. Congratulations," she took our drink orders and walked toward the kitchen.

After our lemonade and iced tea arrived, we held our drinks, reached across the table, clinked glasses, and Mom said, "To the new graduate." Throughout the meal, we took turns recalling various roadblocks and challenges over the last year, and we each shared the relief we felt at the ultimate triumph of getting that high school diploma. *We laughed, joking that maybe we should write a book about the whole experience one day!*

After we finished our entrées, the waitress brought me a surprise dessert plate with vanilla ice cream, whipped cream, and colored sprinkles. The whipped cream spelled out "CONGRATS!"

It was good to put high school behind me—and my focus quickly shifted to college. Was I ready, and if not, how would I get ready? One thing was for sure: I was determined to try and do my best!

As the first day of college approached, I was never more sure and more nervous at the same time. I worked with my mom, and we found the name and contact information of the college disability department. We worked together to set up a meeting with the person in charge of the disability program at the art college. The head of the disability office worked with me on reviewing my high school IEP and creating a new accommodations document specific to my needs for discovering success in college. She said the main difference between high school and college was that I delivered and communicated my accommodations needs. Fortunately, advocating for my accommodations was a skill I was comfortable with.

I understood that getting help from others was a strength, not a weakness.

As soon as I got my college class schedule, I sent out emails to each instructor that included an introduction, my excitement to attend their class and the attachment of my college-approved accommodations. I made sure to cc the disability department head on each email so instructors would know it was all legitimate. I did this for every class, every year, and every grade. Even if I had already had the instructor in a previous class. I often received a response from within the week. The response was either a simple acknowledgment of the information or a request to meet and discuss my accommodation needs in more detail. I felt that the college instructors wanted to understand, and they had the same goal -for me to reach my learning potential.

As the start date for college loomed closer, my elation turned into extreme anxiety—the "what-ifs" in my head were at an all-time high. The anxiety got increasingly out of control; I would even have flashbacks and remember my first day at middle school, being late to every class, never being able to master a locker, and leaving each class more confused. Most of all, I remember feeling that I did not belong and wasn't wanted because I learned differently. I decided to confront the what-ifs one at a time and make a plan for addressing each. For example, what if I was late because the school was so big and I did not know how to find my classes? I decided I would make a plan for this and all of my what-if concerns. Eventually, my anxiety got less, and I felt more in control and confident about starting my college journey.

My nerves were reduced when I started to consider everything I could do to prevent the past from reoccurring. For example, I figured out when the college building was open, and I went on three separate occasions the week before school started to practice walking from the first to the last class listed on my first-semester schedule. With practice, I found and explored each classroom. I checked out the desks and the walls while looking at every option to plug in my laptop. Some rooms took me longer to find as they were tucked way down a hall or on the lower level. Each room was vastly different from the others with its seating options and arrangements. I investigated and became familiar with each room, thinking about where I might sit. For example, sitting near the window wasn't a good option for me as I might become distracted by the outside. I didn't want to get caught in a middle row of seats, and I wanted to be near an outlet. I kept working through my schedule and even found the cafeteria area I might visit if I felt my sugars crashing. This preparation took a little time, but it boosted my confidence!

After my practice run, I felt so much better and was again looking forward to the first day of art college.

Until one night, I dreamt I would be late for my classes because the halls were full of people.

I decided to go back to the college and explore different routes, including where all the stairs were located. I returned to the art school and discovered there were four stairwells in total—one did not go from top to bottom, but the other three did. This added information relieved me, as I now knew I had options if there were too many people or if my planned path was blocked for some reason.

This additional visit added to my confidence, and then I noticed, as I was on my way to leave, a long hall of lockers. Combination locks were my nemesis. For some reason, I just couldn't master the combination lock to save my life. Just like in high school, I would simply carry all my books to each class, even if it meant carrying two full backpacks each day.

The weekend before school started, I spent eight hours on Saturday going through all my clothes and putting together outfits I could comfortably sit and move in. I tried on each outfit for its fit, comfort, and look. I couldn't afford to waste any time in the morning or evening figuring out a daily outfit to wear. I was feeling ready; all my what-ifs were checked off. I can do this!

MOM'S PERSPECTIVE:

In my experience, navigating the adult world takes a lot of skills to thrive. Balancing schedules, keeping up with healthcare needs, sustaining household chores, supporting school needs, and managing employment demands takes robust organizing skills, negotiation skills, time management skills, and planning skills to avoid major disruptions. Life skills are abilities for adaptive and positive behavior that allow us to deal effectively with the demands and challenges of life. These skills help us manage bills, track assignments, find a doctor, set appointments, and navigate the route and time to arrive promptly. We discovered and used as many tools as possible to increase Kelly's independence. The reality was that to get the support she needed to do well in college, she would also have to start practicing "Adulting."

Preparing a neurodivergent learner for college was a new experience for both of us. The educational degree Kelly was aiming to achieve was beyond my expertise. She was going to college to get a degree in communication design. She had studied the campus layout and, at first, fantasized about living in the college dorms. I wanted her to experience independence, but living in the dorms was unlike a sleepover. Kelly would have to get used to the expectations of her roommate. She would be responsible for getting up, getting out, and getting back on time, all on her own, and this was not something she had done yet (like many high school students). She would also have to self-manage her medications for the first time. We discussed this as a possibility after her first year's completion and after she felt comfortable navigating the college schedule and balancing the assignment load.

Shortly after the acceptance letter came, I helped her find the disabilities department of the school and set up a meeting. She met with the head of the disabilities department and learned how her current accommodations would or would not be supported in college. The college would approve some accommodations if Kelly had an IEP or a professional diagnosis within the last three years. Fortunately, these requirements were met. She and the department head communicated her accommodation needs and established approval for support from the college. Kelly sent the approved accommodation letter to each teacher after classes were assigned, and many of the teachers wrote back right away with comments of acceptance or asked to meet with her and to understand more.

RESEARCH INFORMATION:

Most colleges encourage students to attend full-time, which can include balancing four to five classes each semester. Determine if this course load is the right decision for your needs. There were some semesters where Kelly worked with her college to finesse a full-time schedule that was distributed equally in the fall, winter, spring, and summer months. This limited her breaks between semesters; however, it balanced her school load to more manageable components. Students may adjust their course load to accommodate their learning abilities, style, and strengths. For example, students can take fewer classes per term if there are more complicated subjects. They can more readily apply tailored learning techniques—like reading lecture transcripts or engaging in online tutorials—when completing course requirements. Students with a particular routine for taking notes during lectures might feel more comfortable following them at home than in the physical classroom. There is no one-size-fits-all, and the neurodivergent student will find a successful balance when they work with their school advisor.

After deciding on the school and schedule, it is equally important to consider and implement plans that complement the various strengths of neurodivergent learning needs. For example, having an accountability partner who works simultaneously in the same room or through video chat can be helpful. Various study videos are available on YouTube to play in the background, including coffee shop music, Study with Me and sounds like brown noise to assist with focus.[1] There are also Pomodoro study technique[2] videos, which have built-in timers for studying and break sessions and are also helpful in avoiding burnout.

REFERENCES:

[1] Mohammad Javad Jafari, Reza Khosrowabadi, Soheila Khodakarim, and Farough Mohammadian. 2019. "The Effect of Noise Exposure on Cognitive Performance and Brain Activity Patterns." *Open Access Macedonian Journal of Medical Sciences* 7 (17): 2924–31. https://doi.org/10.3889/oamjms.2019.742

[2] Sander Tamm. 2023. "The Pomodoro Study Method: A Complete Guide." E-Student. August 28, 2023. https://e-student.org/pomodoro-study-method/.

ACTION ITEMS:

1. Embrace any concerns about beginning something new by mentally or physically walking through each scenario.

2. Ask "what if" for every anxiety, and answer with realistic options. What if that/this happens? Then, I could do Option A, Option B, and Option C.

3. Create a contingency plan for concerns that are high-risk. For example, I will make and review a checklist every day before I leave for school.

ASKING FOR HELP IS A STRENGTH, NOT A WEAKNESS.

CHAPTER 13

NEW WORLD:
EARLY COLLEGE YEARS

T he first day of college starts, and I wake up early. I brush my teeth, put on a preselected outfit, and eat breakfast. It's two hours before school starts. My mom works close to the art college and drops me off at the front of the school an hour before my first class starts. I say, "I love you" and "goodbye" to Mom as she makes me smile and reminds me of the success that got me here. I check in through security and read a sign that says, "Welcome, Students!"

I do not even look at my schedule because I have it memorized. I walk quickly past every person and directly to my first classroom. I go to the chair I picked during my practice run, sit, and wait. Slowly, others come into the classroom, and every chair is filled. I am so glad I got here first. The teacher introduces himself, and we introduce ourselves around the room. It looks like it will be a fun class. The teacher hands out a large plastic portfolio bag filled with art supplies, including a two-foot metal ruler. His assistant gives us each an "assigned locker" with a combination code and tells the class the lockers are located on the building's second floor in the north wing. My phone alarm vibrates, and I know it is time to go to the next class. I put all the items and papers into the big art bag and head toward the stairs to make my way to the next class.

Walking up two flights of stairs with the portfolio bag slows me down, but I am determined. I get to my next classroom on schedule, and no one is there. I sit and wait. My alarm goes off, indicating class is starting. No one is in the room; oh no, I am late! I texted my mom about the situation, and she advised me to look again at the room listed on the online schedule. Help, they changed the room on me. I am off to find the updated new room. The halls are still pretty full, and the new room is only two classes down. I am the last to walk in. I open the door and see that the seats are full except for a few in the front. The instructor says, "Come on in," with a big smile. As I sit down, I want to tell him all the work I did to avoid being late, but I nod and smile as I know he has already started the class. After introductions, this also looks like a fun class. The instructor introduces a software program called Canvas and walks us through where all the assignments will be explained and provides a tutorial that explains how to submit them. I have recorded the information, and I will watch it tonight because he went too fast for me to keep up.

In this same class, we break up into groups and talk about our first assignment. We need to design a website. I like my group, and they seem to like me. As the class concluded and the instructor dismissed us, I put the material handed out for this class in my big portfolio bag. My phone alarm goes off, and I head to my next class. I have a total of five classes and by the end of the day, I am exhausted. I go outside, and my mom is waiting for me. I opened the trunk and the back seat to put in all the material I collected on the first day. My back aches as I get into our family car. I decided that I must figure out how to get a locker even if I can never close it.

The next day, before my afternoon classes start, I locate the accommodations department. I shared with the program director that I need a locker but can not use combination-style locks. She sends someone with me, and we look at the available lockers. After attempting to train me for over 20 minutes, the person does not give up on me and instead says they have another idea. When I finished my afternoon classes, I was delighted that my new locker was modified to have a key lock. This is much easier! As long as I never lose the key, I should be able to save my back, store my stuff, and have my supplies readily available to use in class.

I used the same locker for the next four years and never once lost the key!

MOM'S PERSPECTIVE:

Kelly's dream of attending college—with much work—came true. As Kelly started to get the hang of the new schedule of college experience, I slowly introduced independent responsibilities for her. When I reminded her, she did her laundry and ordered her medication refills. She scheduled some doctor appointments, and sometimes, she felt she did not need me to join her when the nurse called her back to meet the doctor. She knew that if she ever needed help, all she had to do was ask. I was grateful to watch her develop a relationship of trust and compliance with her provider and the healthcare team. There were incidents along the way. For example, one night, she told me she was out of her insomnia medication. She managed to get through and created a backup plan and a new reminder system.

I wish for Kelly to be independent, chase her dreams, and find her unique way to create positive change in her community. She is well on her way with her passion to share her story with others so their path is not as difficult.

I am so proud of who she is and what she has overcome. She has taught me patience and perseverance and that seeing the world differently is not limiting but the very essence of creativity, innovation, strength, and love.

Learning differently is wonderful and should be embraced with our minds wide open to inclusivity and opportunity for equity of learning for all.

RESEARCH INFORMATION:

Maximizing time efficiency and focusing energy on the college degree is a proven strategy. This involves reducing guesswork for what assignments are expected and asking the teacher who assigns the grade regularly and often directly. Many new college students make assumptions or ask peers what they thought the college teacher was requesting for an assignment or inclusion on the exam. This often results in a lower graded result, not because of poor work but because of not following the prompt. It is essential to ask the person who hands out the grade based on their expectations.

Likewise, maximizing time to take in the new college experience is highly recommended. This may mean limiting all social activities so college students can concentrate on their new schedules and assignments. This increases their acclimation to the college studies workload and time allotment for students to create processes and procedures that work for their learning needs. For example, when students start college, they have new devices to learn, new schedules, new software, new buildings to navigate, and new crowds of people to experience. This and new subjects and assignments can happen all in the same timeline of the first week of classes.

One thing to start getting into the habit of is maximizing your time. Minimize the workload and make good judgments when selecting your socialization outings so that you can ensure you don't create crunch time down the line. Also, when there is downtime, and you feel you can concentrate and do quality work, use the time to complete assignments.

It can be frustrating to work hard on a project only to discover you didn't do it correctly. Get in the habit of asking the teacher for clarification to understand the assignment. Kelly discovered it helps to ask for specific examples from previous A-graded students who have completed the assignment successfully. If more clarity is still needed, ask what particular components completed on the A-graded assignment warranted the assigned grade. Your teachers want you to succeed. They should be happy to provide examples so you can do your best.

Take the time to tour the college campus early and find the classes, get accustomed to the physical environment, and navigate the building, including bathrooms and the cafeteria. Schedule intentional time to review the software used at the school for class schedules, assignments, and email accounts. Make the time to prep the study area so it's organized, creating an area with minimal distractions and maximum opportunity to focus. Send an email to every assigned teacher the week before class starts with an introduction, your excitement to take the class, a list of approved accommodations, and a request to view the syllabus.

All other activities or necessities will add to the stress of balancing the priority of school. If you would like or need to work while attending school, it is advisable to either start the new job six months before college starts or wait to start the new job after the first semester of college. While not always financially feasible, the decision minimizes the stress for the first semester, so college life for the neurodivergent learner can be a priority focus.

From reading this book, you've figured out by now that ADHD can be an incredibly frustrating form of neurodiversity because it does not necessarily relate to the student's ability to understand a concept; instead, it inhibits the ability to demonstrate understanding of that concept. This can make it more challenging to complete the course requirements or to learn the concept properly in the first place. This difficulty in keeping focus can manifest itself in many ways, such as having to re-watch a pre-recorded lecture, requiring the student to take more time to complete course requirements and learn a topic. We've listed several resources to benefit college students with ADHD at the back of the book and on our website, Neuro-Naviation.com.

New tools and resources are being developed regularly, so take the time every semester to search for new options that may enhance your neurodivergent learning style.

Selecting the classes that best support your learning style is also recommended. For example, online college degrees are more popular than ever and may better suit some learners. Remote learning provides students unparalleled learning flexibility, allowing them to attend class when they might not otherwise be able to. This flexibility of remote learning can offer a distinct advantage for neurodiverse students. Distance learning formats will vary by school and program, but much of the online college classroom process allows for self-paced and self-directed learning.

ACTION ITEMS:

1. Establish a comprehensive support plan that covers transportation, surprise funding needs (e.g., cash-only cafeteria), navigational challenges, and effective tracking of schedules and assignments.

2. Develop a support guide detailing whom to contact or which office to visit in case of any unexpected issues during the initial weeks of school.

3. Ensure that you have a reliable wingman—one or two trusted individuals who are aware of your current situation and can assist promptly in stressful scenarios (e.g., a missed bus).

IT'S NOT EASY,
AND YET HERE YOU ARE,
MAKING YOUR SUCCESS HAPPEN.

CHAPTER 14

BRIDGING MINDS: CREATING NEURODIVERGENT ALLIES

College was, at first, extremely challenging to understand, navigate, and keep up with. But I felt I belonged! I met several people at college who had varying degrees of neurodivergent learning needs. It is hard to explain, but I feel like neurodivergent individuals can spot each other in a crowd. We stand out to each other, like an emo student at a private school. Mostly, I clicked with others who were neurodivergent like me; we clicked in the ability to respect each other, especially when challenged to understand the schoolwork assignments.

For the first time, I knew what having a group of friends was like. There are six of us, including me, and we each come from vastly diverse backgrounds. We each have at least one specific learning disability, and four of us are diagnosed with ADHD.

I met Ness and Sam in different first-year classes. Sam is an amazing illustrator! Ness introduced Rose and Mari. Before the week was over, Mari introduced Shawn. We call ourselves the "Lady Bears" because we promised to be brutally honest with each other, critiquing everything from communication style to relationships and classroom work. We completely respected each other and wanted each other to succeed. In this relationship, you could tell that each person had nothing but love and honesty in the critiquing process.

We appreciated that when class is out for most group members, four to eight hours are next on our agendas to review the information and work on the assignment. That's just the reality of someone who learns differently. When someone said, "I want to go with you, but I have homework," the others understood. We tried to help each other as much as possible, and there was something comforting about the friend group, where we could genuinely be ourselves and laugh at our weaknesses. When I am with my friends, it feels like home.

At the end of the first year, we were asked to identify our major and minor. There were many choices, and I knew I wanted to do more than just add to my photography skills. I consulted the Lady Bears. Some were going into illustration, another was going into product design, one in architecture, and another was majoring in studio practice, and, honestly, I just wasn't sure where I would fit best. As I worked with instructors and considered my experience of learning challenges over the years, as well as hearing similar challenges from my new friends, I decided I wanted to make a change in how people like me learn in a neurotypical school system. Therefore, for a major, I decided that communication design was the closest to my heart and the most useful one for me to facilitate future positive change.

MOM'S PERSPECTIVE:

Kelly had to adapt, and she struggled the first year as she navigated the college system and the preferred communication style of each teacher while maintaining a full schedule.

Kelly made friends at college but unfortunately also experienced the disconnect of new friends, as many dropped out within the first two years.

Kelly made many sacrifices to do well in college. She rarely went out with friends after school hours or on the weekend due to the time she needed to get assignments completed. To her detriment, Kelly has been a student who must get the best grade possible. She says she must prove she can do every assignment and test well. She does not compete with other students but herself, including her haunting past.

The time spent to accomplish each school semester sometimes makes Kelly feel unbalanced as she neglects self-care. On two occasions during college, she had what I would call meltdowns where she was so stressed due to the pressure of homework assignments that she lost emotional control and physical control for about five long minutes. Each time this happens, it is very worrying to watch as she yells at herself and hits her body. On one occasion, she hit her head so hard, multiple times against the carpeted floor, she managed to give herself a minor concussion. It isn't easy to encourage her to take other outlets to release this frustration while it's happening in real-time, yet it is so painful to watch her do these violent acts to her body.

We all have limits, and this is her experience. She works to regain control much quicker and grasped at other means to relieve the stress, thankfully no longer physically taking it out on her body.

RESEARCH INFORMATION:

According to research from Patrick Dwyer and colleagues from the University of California-Davis, neurodivergent students continue to face severe barriers and challenges on campus despite increasing numbers of them seeking postsecondary education.[1]

Their research also concludes that neurodivergent students often face specific barriers, including lack of awareness, stigma, discrimination, and inflexible policies and practices, which make the process of getting support more difficult. For example, some colleges require students to provide extensive documentation of their disability, which can be costly, time-consuming, and stressful.

Sensory Overload: College campuses are bustling environments. From crowded lecture halls to social gatherings, the constant stimulation can be overwhelming for individuals, especially neurodivergent learners. Sensory sensitivities, such as heightened reactions to lights, sounds, or physical sensations, can make specific campus environments unbearable, affecting students' ability to concentrate or participate fully.

Unfortunately, some colleges also do not recognize sensory distress and distraction as valid reasons for accommodations, such as wearing a noise-canceling device, using fidget toys, or taking breaks. If you find yourself in this situation, gather research, ask for support from the disabilities department, and advocate for your needs.

Communication Barriers: For some neurodivergent individuals, articulating thoughts, feelings, or needs effectively can be complex. Whether it is misunderstanding figurative language, grappling with speech processing delays, or simply finding the right words, these communication hurdles can lead to misinterpretations and missed opportunities for collaboration or connection.

REFERENCE:

[1] D. Peterschmidt. 2022. "Meet Two Autistic Researchers Changing How Autism Research Is Done." Science Friday, September 1, 2022. https://www.sciencefriday.com/segments/autism-research/

ACTION ITEMS:

1. List five accomplishments that originally felt impossible but eventually were achieved. Hang and review this list at least once a week.

2. Find a relief valve. Be creative, learn to crochet, or enjoy the animals in a local park. Find that one thing that gives you joy and a break from the stresses of life.

3. Celebrate your accomplishments. Take intentional time to be extra kind to yourself and celebrate what you make happen. It's not easy, and yet you are creating success!

CREATIVITY AND LOVE COME FROM AUTHENTICITY AND INCLUSIVITY.

CHAPTER 15

BEAUTIFULLY DIFFERENT: FINDING MY PASSION

I have slowly figured out in my neurodivergent journey the importance of how people communicate with neurodivergent learners, which is dependent on the ability to connect them to the neurotypical world. As I look back, it dawns on me that I have had to be the one to create the bridge to understanding. I have used varying methods to communicate with those who are knowledgeable about information. I see things differently, not just from another perspective but different. When I can express my perspective, I notice others have an appreciation and sometimes seem to be amazed by my description of perception. However, when I cannot communicate the decisions that makeup why the design exists as I see it or as I have created it, the bridge of connections does not work. I selected the major of communication design, and now I have to express my perception of how communication designs can achieve a connection between neurodivergent and neurotypical communities.

During my junior year at college, I completed an independent study on neurodivergent learners. This independent study was purposely aimed at educating others on specific learning disabilities. I wanted to share my experience and what I have learned in my studies on the subject. My goal was to increase awareness of the discrimination and lack of learning equity for neurodivergent learners in the school system. My independent study aimed to identify the history uncovered about the neurodivergent population, create awareness, and build communities. I proudly received an A grade for this work, and I was flattered by the many audience members who shared their appreciation for the information. University staff pulled me aside afterward and asked me to share the study in their classrooms. My study incorporated a timeline I developed, tracing the historical evolution of specific learning disabilities. Additionally, I shared my personal discoveries as a neurodivergent learner.

In addition to a meta-analysis, my study included a school-wide student survey and personal interviews with the staff in charge of the university's disability department. I concluded my independent study with several recommendations for improving equity in education. Many of these are things the college is working on implementing now. These include the introduction of the disabilities department and services provided to all students. The current format requires students to discover the department on their own. Another recommendation was knowledge, access, and support for diagnosis services. Sixty percent of the students surveyed stated they were told within their education systems that they had a learning disability; however, they were never officially diagnosed. Accessing services and being included in the ADA protection often requires an official diagnosis. My complete study is available on our website, Neuro-Navigation.com, and I'll speak more about the complete recommendation list in the next chapter.

But first, I want to say that it seems the more I talk about my journey, the more people come to me for help as they navigate their neurodivergent journey.

For example, Piper, a sophomore, approached me after my independent study presentation and asked for help. I immediately recognized her body language, which showed desperation, frustration, shame, and hopelessness. I sat with her for the next two hours, and she shared that she was taking the same first-year history class for the third time. She felt she could do it this time, yet she saw all the same patterns that happened before. These patterns included failing to understand the assignments correctly, failing to submit work on time, and receiving poor results on the timed exams.

I could see in her eyes that she saw her dream of achieving a college degree slipping between her fingers. I started to ask questions: Do you have a learning disability? What about ADHD? Have you been diagnosed? Have you heard of accommodations? Are you connecting with each teacher to express your interest in doing your best? Do you feel it would help to have specific tools and resources to succeed, etc.? We then used this information to create a plan. Piper followed the plan, and when I checked in with her later, she started to make up for the work she had fallen behind on. Long story short, she scraped by with a C- and while she worked very hard for it, she was primarily proud that she could continue on her path to earn her bachelor's degree.

In another example, I was sitting at the Christmas table with my family, sharing the excitement of releasing my dyslexia children's book and my goals to reach children and their families as early as possible, when my cousin pulled me aside and shared that he was struggling in college. He is brilliant and wanted to complete a bachelor's degree in chemistry, but because he had never dealt with his ADHD, he dropped out of college. He took a break, and because he didn't want to give up on his dream to learn, he enrolled in community college, but he was seeing similar frustrating results. He asked to know more about my story, so I explained some of my biggest aha! moments and then he opened up and shared his experiences. He asked many questions and finally shared that he needed help, too. We discussed his situation, his next steps, where to seek support, and what tools and resources were available. I appreciated the conversation, which made me realize how much I had to offer due to my first-hand experiences.

I could share so many more stories, and all are unique in their tales of struggle and determination, but they all have a common thread.

My first-hand experiences also help others who are not neurodivergent understand those who are. I met one of my most intimidating college instructors in my sophomore year. When I showed him my accommodation letter, he responded coldly, saying, "That looks like a bunch of excuses not to do the work," and that he didn't believe in accommodations. I cringed. It wasn't the first time I had a teacher who did not want to follow my accommodations.

He had a lecture that week, and I reminded him of my accommodation to record it. He rolled his eyes but allowed me. I was always first to arrive, last to leave, and never missed his class. I sat in the front row and asked questions, and when I could, I answered the ones he asked the class.

When he returned one of my assignments, he shared that he appreciated my persistent intent to learn. Only on one rare occasion when he asked me to read from a PowerPoint did I need to remind him of my learning disabilities, and when I did, he supported me. When I told him I wanted to do more and get an A, he responded that he doesn't give out A's because the amount of work needed to earn it doesn't happen. Nonetheless, I kept asking for extra work, and he eventually gave the class an optional extra credit assignment. It was a grueling 45-minute presentation based on research we had to conduct outside of class. I was the only one who completed the extra assignment.

Fast-forward and he became my favorite and most valued teacher. He shared with me later that he was used to students making excuses, and I shared with him that I was used to teachers not understanding, so we challenged each other to grow. He accepted and respected my accommodations as I showed him how and why I needed them.

Today, I consider him a friend. He gave me the academic confidence I've struggled to achieve all my life. He allowed and even encouraged me to argue with authority when I believed my perspective was fair and true. Three years later, after completing his class, he regularly sends me the latest research on learning disabilities and is one of my biggest supporters. I greatly respect and appreciate him!

When grades were posted at the end of the semester, I was pleased I earned an A- in his class.

All neurodivergent learners deserve the chance to make their academic dreams come true. Neurodivergent learners have a different way of solving problems and contributing to the community. Sharing our unique way of thinking is worth the investment!

I want to share my success and help others find theirs!

MOM'S PERSPECTIVE:

One night, shortly before Kelly started college, I went to bed thinking, this is the bravest person I have ever met! Each day, she is reminded of her disabilities, and yet she continues to persevere. And she does it with empathy and courage to make positive change for all people like her.

Kelly had talked about going to college from a young age, and when she started to figure out how successful reading was, she regularly talked about going to college. I believe she had this notion that she wanted to prove to herself and others that she was clever but just learned differently. I always felt that my job as a parent was to remove as many barriers as possible and help her access the roads she would travel to achieve her dreams. This job was much more involved and challenging than I had ever imagined since the day we received her disability diagnosis, primarily because of my lack of knowledge of how to overcome the barriers that she faced, which included more than just her disabilities.

Not that Kelly's struggles were over, however. They were still very real.

Even after she started to get into the groove with her college expectations, she continued to experience episodes due to her learning disabilities. For example, in a junior year printing class, she was assigned a project to create—and mass-produce—a book using a printing press. This involved lead-type blocks—one per each letter of the alphabet—being aligned on the letterpress. The blocks of letters are placed backward in the printing machine so they are readable when ink is rolled over them and pressed onto the paper. She was anxious because all her peers quickly lined up their letters in the machine and were ready to proceed to the printing step, but after

THE CHILD WHO LEARNED DIFFERENTLY

four hours of rearranging her letters again and again, Kelly just sat on the empty shop floor and cried. No matter how she aligned her letters, her test print revealed at least ten letters backward and sometimes upside down! Kelly shared that after four hours, she was exhausted, and her head hurt from trying so hard to figure it out. She said she regretted not swallowing her pride and asking for help before class was done and all had left. When one of her classmates came back to the room looking for the fob they left behind, Kelly bravely asked for help, and her peer graciously obliged. In minutes, they got the letters corrected together, and she was ready to proceed with the printing steps. Before the peer left, Kelly found the fob sitting on a mouse pad—right where its owner left it.

The experience brought back a flood of emotions for Kelly. She shared that she once again watched others easily accomplish something she could not. While she was thankful for the help from the other student, she expressed with tears in her eyes that it was a harsh reminder of that paralyzing feeling her specific learning disabilities can create.

It broke my heart to hear her tell this story; it had been a long time since we had one of these talks. She said the experience was like a scary nightmare that she thought had disappeared, but it suddenly returned with a vengeance. She said as she sat on the shop floor alone crying, she sensed icy fingers squeezing her heart, a flood of memories of past feelings—like fear, regret, and powerlessness. I praised her for her recovery. "That was then, this is now," I said. I reminded her that she had regained her strength when she got a second chance and jumped on it. While she temporarily felt powerless, she must have still been in control of her emotions and composure, as she did not revert to self-harm. Finally, I shared that her episode sounded exhausting, haunting, and hurtful, yet I couldn't help but be proud of how she found the strength to persevere, rise up, and walk away, knowing she had ultimately achieved success.

She finished her book two weeks ahead of schedule and received an A+ for the assignment.

RESEARCH INFORMATION:

The struggles of neurodivergent college students are reflected in the disparity of graduation rates between students with disabilities and students without disabilities. The six-year graduation rate of students with disabilities at four-year colleges is 49.5%, compared to almost 68% for students without disabilities. According to research by psychologist Susan W. White, only 41% of students with disabilities enrolled in a four-year college will graduate with a bachelor's degree.[1]

The radical increase in the balance of responsibilities experienced by a new first-year student in high school is similar for neurodiverse college students as they will endure additional and unique challenges compared to their neurotypical peers. Getting a college degree is a challenging feat for most. For those who identify as neurodivergent, a leveling of the educational playing field is required to create equity for neurodivergent learners.

The Unique Challenges of Neurodivergent Students in College: For many, college is seen as a launchpad to adulthood, filled with new experiences, friendships, and personal growth. However, the very factors that make college exciting can also make it daunting, particularly for neurodivergent students. Their unique cognitive wiring, while a source of many strengths, can also introduce specific challenges in the conventional college setting.

Understanding Social Nuances: College is not just about studying. It is also about building friendships, joining clubs, and networking. For those with ASD or NVLD, understanding social cues and nuances might not always come naturally. While it can be expected for neurotypical individuals to speak with hints or come from a sense of sarcasm, these communication clues can be confusing for some neurodivergent learners. Potential misinterpretations can lead to feelings of isolation and frustration.

Executive Functioning Struggles: Organizing notes, managing time, sticking to schedules, and other essential skills, known as executive functions, are often tricky for neurodivergent students. Traditional colleges emphasizing self-directed study can add additional triggers and worsen these challenges.

Inadequate Support: While colleges may offer some support for students with disabilities, the specific support functions do not always cater specifically to the needs of the neurodivergent population. Generic accommodations may not address the unique challenges these students face.

Even with a college degree, there are challenges for those who learn differently. While the unemployment rate for people with disabilities drops with higher levels of education, bachelor's degree holders with disabilities face higher unemployment rates than those without disabilities. According to the Bureau of Labor Statistics, the unemployment rate for people with disabilities is about double that for people without disabilities (7.6% vs. 3.5%).[2]

REFERENCES:

[1] Joshua Pretlow, Deonte Jackson, Michael Bryan, and RTI International. 2020. "A 2017 Follow-up: Six-Year Persistence and Attainment at First Institution for 2011–12 First-time Postsecondary Students." NCES 2020-237. **https://nces.ed.gov/pubs2020/2020237.pdf**.

[2] "Persons With a Disability: Labor Force Characteristics - 2023 A01 Results." n.d. https://www.bls.gov/news.release/disabl.toc.htm.

ACTION ITEMS:

1. Create an accommodation list for all areas of life's success, including work, school, and community activities. Share this list with the department responsible for disability inclusion. We have posted some examples on our website, Neuro-Navigation.com.

2. Practice self-advocacy and strength in both written and verbal communication. We have a list of examples in the back of the book and update them regularly on our Neuro-Navigation.com website.

3. Discover communities that support and embrace neurodivergent learners.

TODAY'S STEPS ADD TO YOUR MOUNTAIN OF ACCOMPLISHMENTS!

CHAPTER 16

FROM PAIN TO PURPOSE: AMPLIFYING THE SILENCED PLEA

I made it! I am doing what my public high school counselor said was "Unlikely." I am graduating college today. Not only am I graduating, but I have also made the President's Honor List four years in a row, and I've been asked to speak at today's graduation ceremony.

I am nervous, but I am ready! I've come a long way from being illiterate at 14. My journey here was more complicated than it had to be, and I'm so grateful to those who believed in me along the way. I had many neurodivergent peers along the way, but sadly, none will be joining me here today on this graduation stage.

The curtain sways slightly in the breeze as I peek around it. I think about my communication design degree and my minor in natural science. While I'm passionate about these degrees, I'm also passionate about helping other neurodivergent learners navigate the education system to achieve their dreams. I fought to be here and have learned so much along the way! I plan to share my experiences, recommendations, and successes with others so that they might find success, too.

[PRESIDENT: … and it's my pleasure to welcome Kelly to the stage.]

I take a deep breath as I walk behind the red velvet curtain and onto the wooden stage. I hear my inner voice say, "Let's do this!"

MY GRADUATION SPEECH: "AMPLIFYING THE SILENCED PLEA."

Friends, esteemed faculty, proud parents, my fellow graduates, and you, the reader, welcome to graduation day!

Today, we stand on the precipice of a new chapter, ready to embark on journeys of our own making. As we reflect on our experiences, we are filled with many emotions—pride, excitement, perhaps a hint of apprehension. Above all, we are filled with gratitude—gratitude for the opportunities afforded to us, gratitude for the support of our loved ones, and gratitude for the chance to defy the odds.

My journey to this podium has been anything but conventional. At the age of 14, I was labeled as "illiterate" by a system that couldn't comprehend the unique way my brain processed information. For years, I struggled to navigate a world that seemed built for minds unlike my own. But I refused to accept the limitations imposed upon me. With determination and the support of those who understood and cared, I began to carve out my own path—a path to achieve equity in my education.

Today, as I stand before you as a graduate on the President's Honor Student List, I am living proof of the power of perseverance and the importance of embracing neurodiversity. My journey serves as a reminder that intelligence takes many forms, and the traditional metrics of success often fail to capture the brilliance that lies within each of us.

But my story is just one of many. Across the nation, countless individuals like myself are navigating a world that does not always understand or accept our differences. Too often, our education system prioritizes conformity over creativity and uniformity over uniqueness. It is a system that leaves behind those who learn differently, perpetuating cycles of exclusion and inequality. For those of us who are neurodivergent, this results in inequity in education, barriers to accomplishing our maximum potential, and silenced pleas for classroom help.

But it doesn't have to be this way.

As we stand on the cusp of the future, we have a responsibility to advocate for change— change that prioritizes learning equity and celebrates the diversity of human cognition. We must challenge the status quo, dismantle barriers to access, amplify the silent pleas for classroom help, and foster environments that embrace neurodiversity as a strength rather than a weakness.

To the educators in the room, I implore you to approach each student with empathy and understanding, to recognize that brilliance knows no bounds, and to champion inclusive teaching practices that empower every learner to thrive.

To my fellow graduates, I urge you to carry the torch of advocacy forward, to be allies to those whose voices have been silenced, and to work toward a future where all individuals are valued and respected for who they are.

To society as a whole, I ask for open-mindedness, compassion, and a willingness to reimagine our education system in a way that honors every child's unique strengths.

As we embark on this next chapter of our lives, let us remember that true progress is not measured solely by academic achievement but by the strides we take toward a more inclusive and equitable world. Together, let us be the architects of change, building a future where neurodiversity is not only accepted—but celebrated.

Congratulations! Our journey is just beginning, and through embracing neurodiversity, the possibilities are endless.

EPILOGUE

Kelly and I never imagined that we would be able to transcribe this painful journey into words. After all, we had been in survival mode for the past twenty years, and pausing to look back was not exactly appealing or practical. However, as we shared triumphs with others in similar situations, we realized that we could help many people by telling our truth in the form of a book—no matter the vulnerability exposed.

We drove into the emotionally tumultuous process of reviewing documents and recounting incidents, memories of extreme desperation, loss of hope and courage, a sense of devastation, overwhelming distress, feelings of abandonment and loneliness, and absolute exhaustion—and we have resurfaced with a vengeance. We exposed personal scars that were thought to be healed and further realized the journey we survived was more traumatic than initially identified while we stumbled through it.

Was it worth it? Yes!

Writing the book was therapeutic and humbling as we often thought of other neurodivergent learners we met who did not have positive outcomes. Fortunately, this book has already served as a guiding light, offering hope and making the path smoother for others. This inspirational story, told from a neurodivergent learner's perspective with the support of her mother, spotlights the fact that the current standardized school system has room for improvement. The current "one-size-fits-all" approach leaves the neurodivergent child behind. This book offers a new way of thinking for education systems that want every student to reach their academic potential.

Exposing the vulnerable yet pivotal experiences that transformed Kelly, a neurodivergent learner, from being illiterate at the age of 14 to graduating college and becoming a published author reveals how a system designed to educate dismissed her needs and passed her from one grade to the next with a trajectory toward homelessness.

Silenced Plea: The Child Who Learned Differently gets to the heart of the need for a change. It is a long-overdue, much-needed answer from the source of truth. Sharing authentic experiences in a system that overlooks, creates limits, and can potentially destroy the lives of those who learn differently.

More than merely embracing being different, neurodivergent learners have value in contributing to society and creating positive changes for the greater good of all. They deserve access to education that embraces their learning style and allows them to reach their maximum potential.

Don't let the world continue to miss out on what neurodivergent learners have to offer!

APPENDIX

STANDARD TESTS USED TO DIAGNOSIS

Standard tests to diagnose a learning disability include intelligence, achievement, visual-motor integration, and language. Intelligence tests (often called IQ tests) most commonly used to diagnose a learning disability include the Wechsler Preschool and Primary Scale of Intelligence (WIPPSI), the Wechsler Intelligence Scale for Children (WISC), and the Wechsler Adult Intelligence Scale (WAIS). Standard achievement tests used to diagnose a learning disability include the Woodcock-Johnson Tests of Achievement (WJ), the Wechsler Individual Achievement Test (WIAT), the Wide Range Achievement Test (WRAT), and the Kaufman Test of Educational Achievement (KTEA). Standard visual motor integration tests include the Bender Visual Motor Gestalt Test and the Developmental Test of Visual Motor Integration.

Language tests are also used to diagnose learning disabilities.

The following are examples of clinical tests that clinicians use to diagnose dyslexia:

- **Clinical Evaluation of Language Fundamentals -5 (CELF-5):** This test provides an overview of oral language and parses out receptive and expressive language skills. It is beneficial in identifying a receptive-expressive language gap.

- **Comprehensive Assessment of Spoken Language (CASL):** This test assesses higher-level language skills, such as figurative language and abstract reasoning.

- **Comprehensive Test of Phonological Processing -2 (CTOPP-2):** This test assesses phonological awareness, memory, and rapid naming.

- **Expressive One-Word Picture Vocabulary Test -4 (EOWPVT-4):** This test assesses expressive vocabulary.

- **Gray Oral Reading Test -5 (GORT-5)** assesses oral reading accuracy, fluency, and comprehension.

- **Gray Silent Reading Test (GSRT)** assesses silent reading comprehension.

- **Rapid Automatic Naming/Rapid Automatic Stimulus (RAN/RAS):** This test assesses the ability to name objects or colors quickly.

- **Test of Auditory Processing Skills (TAPS):** This test assesses auditory processing skills such as memory and discrimination.

- **Test of Early Written Language (TEWL):** This test assesses early writing skills such as letter formation and spelling.

- **Test of Pragmatic Language (TOPL):** This test assesses pragmatic language skills such as social communication and problem-solving.

- **Test of Written Language -4 (TOWL-4):** This test assesses written expression skills such as sentence combining and contextual conventions.

- **Test of Written Spelling -5 (TWS-5):** This test assesses spelling skills.

- **Woodcock Reading Mastery Test (WRMT)** assesses word identification, word attack skills, and passage comprehension.

- **Word Test:** This test assesses word recognition speed and accuracy

AN EXAMPLE OF "ABOUT ME"

The template can be downloaded from www.neuro-navigation.com.

 neuro About me:
NAVIGATION

School: Perry Elementary Class: Social studies Teacher: Mrs. Dobbs Semester/Year: Fall/2023

Dear Teacher,

I'm a neurodivergent student. This means I learn differently than how things are typically taught. I'm still working to figure out what works best for my comprehension, retention and understanding of school concepts. I've provided below what I know so far. I look forward to learning more with you!

Signed: Kelly V.

My Name: Kelly VanZant
Preferred name: Kelly
Pronouns: She/her/hers
Learning Style: Visual

Some of the things I'm good at:

I'm good at putting puzzles together and asking lots of questions to figure out puzzle games. I'm a really good swimmer and can jump off the high diving board. I am a loving and kind person, and I have won many awards from my photography

Some of the things I enjoy:

I enjoy taking pictures with my camera. Something I can do that I'm really proud of is growing and picking strawberries in my garden. I like to kayak with my mom and go on long hikes. I like roasting marshmallows on a campfire. I really like snuggling my cat.

I could use your help at:

Making new friends

Sitting in front of class so I can pay attention

Being allowed to get rid of my excess energy so I can pay attention

Getting reminders on where to go next during and after class

Not being asked to suddenly read/write in front of my peers

My challenges:

Remembering more than one task or concept at the same time

Reading at my grade level

Writing at my grade level

Keeping friends due to not understanding social ques or their lack of understanding that I learn differently

Learning how to whisper

What I'm working on and how others can help:

Listening skills, others can help by offering to repeat when asked or confirming my understanding of information shared

Advocating for myself, others can help by asking if I have what I need or if they can provide more information/support for my learning success

Understanding my learning differences and how to work with them, others can help by being patient in explaining concepts, offering different tools or resources for my understanding efforts, reminding me that I am clever and praising me for what I accomplish and when I don't give up

ADVOCATE STRATEGIES FOR STUDENTS WITH ATTENTION DEFICITS:

- **Communicate regularly:** When parents periodically communicate with their child's teacher about problems and progress, the child's interests have a better chance of remaining a top priority for all who care about them. It is essential to document these conversations with data, who was present, key issues, and action items for the next steps.

- **Observe and stay connected**: Parents should observe and talk with their child about what helps or distracts them (for example, fidget tools, brown noise, or pencil adaptors). As you find tools that work, don't forget to ask the school if they can supply or supplement the cost of the item.

- **Organization support**: Discover how to best organize papers for evening homework and prepare for the next school day. This can be done using colored pocket folders assigned to the classroom or the day due. Let the teacher know about your system so they can support its success.

It is important to note that children with attention deficits experience more obstacles in their path to success than the average student. Your regular reminders of love and support for their success will go a long way as they learn what works best for them to be successful.

IEP BASICS:

At a minimum, an Individual Education Plan must include:

The child's present levels of academic achievement and functional performance, the impact of the child's disability on their involvement and progress in the general education curriculum, goals aligned with grade-level content standards for all children with disabilities, the use of positive behavioral interventions and supports, and other strategies to address behavior as needed,

And a statement from the special education lead on their related services and supplementary aids to be provided to the child. Students with IEP (Individualized Education Program) have several diploma options based on their unique needs and educational plans. Here are the main types of diplomas they may receive:

1. IEP/Special Education Diploma: This option is specifically designed for students receiving special education services and those with IEP. The requirements for this diploma are usually set by the student's IEP team and are tailored to each individual.

2. Occupational Diploma: Students enrolled in vocational programs may receive this type of diploma. It recognizes their specialized training and skills in a specific occupational field.

3. Applied Studies Diploma: Available to students who receive modifications under an IEP, this diploma acknowledges their achievements and adaptations in the educational setting.

Remember that each state may have unique graduation requirements and diploma options, so it's essential to consult local guidelines for specific details. These diploma options ensure that students with disabilities can successfully complete their high school education and transition to their next steps in life.

People with disabilities who hold an IEP diploma may face challenges in finding employment opportunities. Employers may not always be familiar with the IEP diploma, which can impact hiring decisions.